Algorithm Animation

ACM Distinguished Dissertations

1982
Abstraction Mechanism and Language Design
Paul N. Hilfinger
Formal Specification of Interactive Graphics Programming Language
William R. Mallgren
Algorithmic Program Debugging
Ehud Y. Shapiro

1983
The Measurement of Visual Motion
Ellen Catherine Hildreth
Synthesis of Digital Designs from Recursion Equations
Steven D. Johnson

1984
Analytic Methods in the Analysis and Design of Number-Theoretic Algorithms
Eric Bach
Model-Based Image Matching Using Location
Henry S. Baird
A Geometric Investigation of Reach
James U. Korein

1985
Two Issues in Public-Key Cryptography
Ben-Zion Chor
The Connection Machine
W. Daniel Hillis

1986
All the Right Moves: A VLSI Architecture for Chess
Carl Ebeling
The Design and Evaluation of a High Performance Smalltalk System
David Michael Ungar

1987
Algorithm Animation
Marc H. Brown
The Rapid Evaluation of Potential Fields in Particle Systems
Leslie Greengard

Algorithm Animation

Marc H. Brown

The MIT Press
Cambridge, Massachusetts
London, England

Publisher's Note

This format is intended to reduce the cost of publishing certain works in book form and to shorten the gap between editorial preparation and final publication. Detailed editing and composition have been avoided by photographing the text of this book directly from the author's prepared copy.

Printed and bound in the United States of America.

Library of Congress Cataloging-in-Publication Data

Brown, Marc H.
  Algorithm animation.

  (ACM distinguished dissertations ; 1987)
  Bibliograpy: p.
  Includes index.
  1. Electronic digital computers—Programming.
2. Algorithms. 3. Computer graphics. I. Title.
II. Series.
QA76.6.B765   1988   006.6   88-10036
ISBN 0-262-02278-8

To Ellen:

My best-friend and lover,
  mi dushi and wife.

אֵשֶׁת חַיִל מִי יִמְצָא
וְרָחֹק מִפְּנִינִים מִכְרָהּ.

And to our parents

Contents

Preface

An algorithm animation environment is a means for exploring the dynamic behavior of algorithms that makes possible a fundamental improvement in the way we understand and think about them. It presents multiple graphical views of an algorithm in action, exposing properties that might otherwise be difficult to understand or even remain unnoticed. All views are updated simultaneously in real time as the algorithm executes, and each view is displayed in a separate window on the screen, whose location, size, and level of detail is interactively set by the end-user. A specialized interpreter controls execution in units that are specific to the algorithm, and allows multiple algorithms to be run simultaneously for comparisons. Programmers can implement new algorithms, graphical displays, and input generators and run them with existing libraries of such components.

An important aspect of an algorithm animation environment, and one we believe is useful in any interactive environment, is the concept of a *script*: a record of an end-user's session that can be replayed. Scripts can be used both passively, as virtual videotapes, and actively, as an innovative communication medium: the viewer of a script can customize the videotape interactively, and can readily switch between passively viewing it and actively exploring its contents. Scripts are typically used as high-level macros, system tutors, and electronic textbooks and research notes. End-users can create scripts easily by instructing the system to "watch what I do;" scripts are stored as readable and editable PASCAL programs.

The potential of such algorithm animation environments is great, but can be fully realized only if they are sufficiently easy and enjoyable to use. This dissertation is step towards achieving these goals. In it, we develop a model for creating real-time animations, as well as a framework for interacting with these animations. We also describe a prototype system, BALSA–II, and its feasibility study system, BALSA–I, that realize the conceptual model.

Acknowledgements

I've looked forward to writing this page for quite some time, having spent over a decade at Brown—as an undergraduate, TA, RA, staff member, and most recently, at the bottom of the totem pole, as a graduate student. My mentors merit more than the "thanks" that an acknowledgement page provides. Yet what does one say?

Bob Sedgewick has gone beyond a mere thesis advisor, professor or colleague. He has provided lodging and repasts—from Marly-le-Roi to Quonochontaug—7am squash matches, incisive interpretations of intra and interdepartmental matters, and a plethora of stimulating intellectual challenges. Sedge sets high standards for himself and those around him, and, more than anyone I know, appreciates one's obsessions for detail and perfection.

My competence as a programmer can be attributed, in part, to fundamental concepts drilled in Andy van Dam's freshman introductory programming course. Throughout the years, Andy's indefatigability, acumen, and vigorous leadership have inspired me and many other students to set high personal goals and to go after them. Computer science needs more people with Andy's genuine love for teaching and undaunted confidence in undergraduates.

The third member of my thesis committee, Paris Kanellakis, epitomizes the word "mensch." His encouragement, keen insight into technical matters, and careful reading of the final draft have been invaluable.

Many thanks to the people who read parts of this thesis for their perceptive comments. In particular, the prose has been greatly improved by two meticulous passes by Trina Avery, and by Cynthia Hibbard's patience and perseverance in explaining to me many intricacies of the English language. Special thanks to DAW for reacquainting me with [63] and for many inspired harangues and motivating discussions. Rob Rubin provided an exceptional sounding board, and frequently painted the global picture for me when I became myopic.

This thesis is an outgrowth of the Electronic Classroom project at Brown, initiated by Bob Sedgewick. The project realizes his vision of bringing "interactive movies" into computer science education and the study of algorithm. Bob, along with Andy van Dam and Tom Doeppner, procured the project's initial funding from NSF's CAUSE program in June, 1980. The Exxon Education Foundation and Apollo Computer provided additional funding.

Literally thousands of computer science students at Brown have taken courses in the Electronic Classroom using the BALSA–I environment. Many people, too numerous to mention here, have contributed to that software endeavor. In particular, Steve Reiss, with some help from Joe Pato and myself, developed the Brown Workstation Environment and tailored it to BALSA–I's requirements. Perry Busalacchi, Ham Lord, Karen Smith, Kate Smith, and Liz Waymire wrote many of the initial BALSA–I animations at a time when the system was unstable, under development, and without documentation. Mike Strickman implemented much of the BALSA–I kernel, Dave Nanian implemented its tools for broadcasting, and Eric Wolf implemented its code view. The hardware and system software was adeptly managed by Dave Durfee, Jeff Coady, and Dorinda Moulton. Their professionalism kept me (and others) in check during many hectic times.

Special credit is due to Bob Sedgewick for his many contributions to this thesis. While I can take full credit for the BALSA–I and BALSA–II systems design and implementation (subject to the acknowledgements cited above), neither system would have reached fruition without Bob's support and feedback. Jointly, we created the first sophisticated set of views and scripts using BALSA–I. Our experiences were instrumental in incremental improvements to BALSA–I and the entire design of BALSA–II. Appendix A discusses this experience and also Andy's experiences as instructor of an Introductory Programming course that used the Electronic Classroom at the same time.

Thus, it is important for readers to understand that when I use the pronoun "we" in this dissertation, it is more than the proverbial "royal we."

Most of the research reported here was performed while I was supported by an IBM Graduate Student Fellowship. My tenure as a graduate student was also supported in part by the ONR and DARPA under Contract N00014–83–K–0146 and ARPA Order No. 4786, and NSF Grant SER80–04974. Their assistance is gratefully acknowledged.

Finally, I am very thankful to Bob Taylor at DEC's Systems Research Center for providing support during the final months. His managerial style and motivation techniques (read: prohibiting me from participating in SRC projects until my dissertation is signed, sealed, and delivered) are creative. I hope my contributions to the SRC environment in the coming years will justify the confidence he has demonstrated.

1

Introduction

An algorithm animation environment is an "exploratorium" for investigating the dynamic behavior of programs, one that makes possible a fundamental improvement in the way we understand and think about them. It presents multiple graphical displays of an algorithm in action, exposing properties of the program that might otherwise be difficult to understand or might even remain unnoticed. All views of the algorithm are updated simultaneously in real time as the program executes; each view is displayed in a separate window on the screen, whose location and size is controlled by the end-user. The end-user can zoom into the graphical (currently, two-dimensional) image to see more detailed information, and can scroll the image horizontally and vertically. Views can also be used for specifying input to programs graphically. A specialized interpreter controls execution in units that are meaningful for the program, and allows multiple algorithms to be run simultaneously for comparing and contrasting. The end-user can control how the algorithms are synchronized by manipulating the amount of time each unit takes to execute. Programmers can implement new algorithms, graphical displays, and input generators and run them with existing libraries of algorithms, displays, and inputs.

While an algorithm animation environment is a rich environment for actively exploring algorithms, in many situations a passive, guided approach using a prepared "script" is more appropriate. For example, when dynamic material is a visual aid in a lecture or when it complements a traditional textbook or journal article, the audience is interested in viewing the "virtual videotape" as the author conceived it, not in exploring the material independently. And when an algorithm is being viewed for the first time, self-guided exploration can easily result in distorted or incorrect interpretations and leave important aspects of the algorithm undiscovered.

To a first approximation, an algorithm animation script is a record of an end-user's session that can be replayed. At one end of the spectrum, a script is merely a videotape that can be viewed passively. At the other, more interesting end of the spectrum, a script is an innovative communication medium: the viewer of a script can customize the movie interactively, and can readily switch between passively viewing it and actively exploring its contents. Scripts can be used as high-level macros, thereby extending the set of commands available to end-users of the algorithm animation system, and can also serve as the basis for broadcasting one end-user's session to other end-users on other machines. End-users can create scripts easily by instructing the system to "watch what I do." Scripts are stored as readable and editable PASCAL programs.

Systems for algorithm animation can be realized with current hardware: personal workstations—with their high-resolution displays, powerful dedicated processors, and large amounts of real and virtual memory—can support the required interactiveness and dynamic graphics. In the future, such workstations will become cheaper, faster, and more powerful, and will have better resolution. An algorithm animation environment exploits these characteristics, and can also take advantage of a number of features expected to become common in future hardware, such as color, sound, and parallel processors.

We develop here a model for creating real-time animations of algorithms with minimal intrusions into the algorithm's original source code, as well as a framework for interacting with these animations. We also describe a prototype system, BALSA–II, and its feasibility study system, BALSA–I, that realize the conceptual model. Currently, BALSA–II is being used in teaching parts of a data structures course, for research in the design and analysis of algorithms, and for technical drawings in research papers and textbooks. BALSA–I has been in production use since 1983 in Brown University's "Electronic Classroom." Appendix A documents some of our experiences using the environment as a principal mode of communication during lectures in an introductory programming course and in an algorithms and data structures course. Appendix B cites publications describing various aspects of the project.

1.1 Thesis Contributions

The primary contributions of this thesis are its models for (1) programmers creating animations, (2) end-users interacting with the animations, and (3) end-users creating, editing, and replaying dynamic documents. These models have been realized in the BALSA–I and BALSA–II systems. A secondary contribution of this research is the numerous static and dynamic graphical displays of a wide range of algorithms and data structures we have created using the prototype systems, most of which had never been displayed or even conceived previously. The domain includes sorting, searching, string processing, parsing, graphs, trees, computational geometry, mathematics, linear and dynamic programming, systolic architectures, and graphics. The systems have also be used to show innovative dynamic illustrations of fundamental concepts in procedural programming languages. The diagrams in this document are a small sampling of these images; others have been reported elsewhere [16, 17, 18].

We now elaborate on the primary contributions of this thesis.

(1) **A model for programmers creating animations.** The programmer model is independent of the contents of all algorithms, inputs and views; hence, it can be used to animate any algorithm in a systematic manner. Moreover, the model makes it easy to animate new algorithms and create new displays.

Algorithms being animated are separated into three components: the *algorithm* itself, an *input generator* that provides data for the algorithm to manipulate, and graphical *views* that present the animated pictures of the algorithm in execution. Views are built following a classical graphics *modeler–renderer* paradigm, and an *adapter* allows any particular view to be used to display aspects of many different algorithms. Modelers can be chained to provide views of views, and renderers can be based on multiple modelers. Algorithms are annotated with *interesting events* to indicate phenomena of interest that should give rise to the displays being updated; in addition, the events provide the abstraction for end-users to control the execution.

(2) **A model for end-users interacting with animated algorithms.** The end-user model, like the programmer model, is independent of the algorithms, inputs, and views; thus, end-users interact with animations

in a consistent manner. This model gives well-defined semantics for each end-user command; in fact, BALSA–I and BALSA–II can be thought of as merely two different user interfaces that manipulate these properties.

The interactive environment is characterized at any point by its *structural, temporal* and *presentation* properties. The structural properties are the set of algorithms currently running and the data they are processing. Information concerning the specialized interpreter, such as the program-specific units chosen for stopping and stepping points and how multiple algorithms are synchronized, are the temporal properties. The configuration of view windows on the screen are considered the presentation properties. In addition to providing data for algorithms to process, end-users can manipulate the underlying algorithms, input generators and views through the concept of *parameters* for each component. That is, end-users can select among parameters preset by the programmers; end-users cannot create new variants at runtime.

(3) **Model for end-users creating, editing, and replaying dynamic documents.** Dynamic documents, called *scripts*, are created by having the system watch what the end-user does. However, a semantic interpretation of the actions is maintained in a textual file—an executable PASCAL program—not a command or keystroke history. Scripts form a basis for passively watching the dynamic material like a videotape, or actively interacting with the material. The script model is mostly independent of an algorithm animation system: the principals can be applied to virtually any system with well-defined structural, temporal and presentation properties.

1.2 Applications of Algorithm Animation

An obvious application of an algorithm animation environment is computer science *instruction*, particularly courses dealing with algorithms and data structures, e.g., compilers, graphics, databases, algorithms, programming. Rather than using a chalkboard or viewgraph to show static diagrams, instructors can present simulations of algorithms and programming concepts on workstations. Moreover, students can try out the programs on their own data, at their own pace, and with different displays (from a library of existing displays) from those the instructor chose. Non-naive students can code their own algorithms and utilize the same set of displays used by the instructor in demonstration programs. As mentioned earlier, the appendices describe how BALSA–I was used in computer science instruction.

Another proven application of an algorithm animation environment is as a tool for *research* in algorithm design and analysis. Human beings' ability to quickly process large amounts of visual information is well documented, and animated displays of algorithms provide intricate details in a format that allows us to exploit our visual capabilities. For instance, experimenting with an animation of Knuth's dynamic Huffman trees [43] revealed strange behavior of the tree dynamics with a particular set of input. This lead to a new, improved algorithm for dynamic Huffman trees [70]. A variation of Shellsort was discovered in conjunction with static color displays of Bubblesort, Cocktail-Shaker Sort, and standard Shellsort [41]. An early version of BALSA–I was used to help understand and analyze a newly discovered stable Mergesort [36].

Animations developed for instruction can be used for research, and vice versa. For example, animations for an algorithms course were used with minor changes to investigate shortest-path algorithms in Euclidean graphs [61]. Conversely, displays developed in conjunction with research on pairing heaps [29] were later incorporated into classroom lectures on priority queues.

Another application for an algorithm animation environment is as a testbed for *technical drawings* of data structures. It allows interactive experimentation with input data and algorithm parameters to produce a picture that best illustrates the desired properties. Furthermore, the drawings produced are always accurate, even ones which would tax the best of draftsmen. For example, it is laborious indeed for a draftsman to take a set of points and prepare the sequence in Figure 1.1 showing the construction of a Voronoi diagram and its dual. As more and more researchers begin to typeset their own papers and books, this application will become increasingly important.

A prime but so far unexplored application area for algorithm animation is in *programming environments*. Pioneering environments on graphics-based workstations, such as Cedar [65], Interlisp [64], and especially Smalltalk [31], are, by and large, text-oriented. Recent workstation-based program development environments incorporate graphical views of the program structure and code, not data, and consequently have had limited success in giving additional insight into the programs: "The experience we have had with

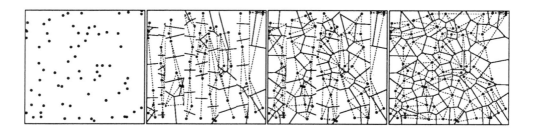

Figure 1.1: *Construction of a Voronoi diagram.*

PECAN, however, has shown that such graphical views are limited in their power and usefulness when they are tied to syntax. The syntactic basis forces the user to treat these two-dimensional representations in a one-dimensional way, and the graphics do not provide any significant advantage over text" [57]. These systems could be greatly enhanced by the display capabilities of an algorithm animation environment.

Algorithm animation has also been used for *performance tuning* [24], and has the potential to be helpful in *documenting programs* [47] and in *systems modeling*, especially for multi-threaded applications.

1.3 Conceptual Model

Algorithm animation involves two types of users: *end-users* and *client-programmers*. The end-users watch and interact with the animations on a workstation, whereas the programmers implement the algorithms, displays, and input generators that the end-users see and manipulate. An algorithm animation system itself is domain-independent: the system does not know whether an algorithm sorts numbers or produces random numbers, or whether a view shows a tree or a table. It does not attempt to decide what phenomena are interesting in a program, or what styles of input or visual representations are appropriate. Rather, it provides tools so that a large variety can be easily implemented and end-users can watch and interact with them in a consistent manner.

We will use the terms *algorithm animation environment* and *algorithm animation system* to reflect the two types of users. The algorithm animation system is the code with which client-programmers interface, and the algorithm animation environment is the runtime environment that end-users see. It is the result of compiling the code that client-programmers implement with the algorithm animation system.

For end-users, the main goal of the algorithm animation environment is to provide a consistent manner in which to interact with animations, independent of who happened to prepare the animation and what domain the animation happens to be from. Once an end-user has used the system for one algorithm, he should know how to use it for any and all algorithms.

For client-programmers, the main goal of an algorithm animation system is to provide all of the ancillary functions needed to make an interactive animation. Each programmer should not need to reinvent and reimplement facilities common to all views, such as zooming into displays. A second important goal is to provide a model whereby the animation code is separated from the algorithm. Moreover, the code relating to the animation (and to preparing input for an algorithm) should be shareable by many algorithms. Thus, a programmer implementing an algorithm should be able to concentrate primarily on the algorithm, independent of input generators and displays and the window configuration selected by the end-user. Conversely, a programmer implementing a display should do so without concern for the algorithm, input generators or the end-users.

The program being animated must be split into various pieces so that the algorithm animation system, as well as the end-users, can manipulate them systematically. Programs are separated into three components: the *algorithm* itself, the various *input generators* that provide data for the algorithm to manipulate, and the various *graphical displays*, or *views*, that present the animated pictures of the algorithm in execution.

The remainder of this section presents a high-level overview of the model an algorithm animation systems gives to its two types of users. The descriptions of the models here are necessarily brief and incomplete; Chapters 3 and 4 are devoted to end-users, and Chapters 5 and 6 to programmers.

End-User's Model

The end-user of an algorithm animation environment is always in a "setup-run" loop:

Setup: The end-user arranges the screen and decides which algorithms to run, which input generator and views to use, and what the values of any parameters to each of these should be. Each algorithm has a default setup that can be designated and changed by the end-user.

Run: The end-user runs the algorithms and watches them in the view windows on the screen. While the algorithms are running, the end-user can suspend them to change the ensemble of views on the screen as well as the program's speed and breakpoints.

Changing or creating the content of an algorithm, view, and input generator is done, strictly speaking, not by an end-user but by a programmer. Such editing is done outside of the algorithm animation environment, using the standard editors and compilers. If the machine supports multiple processes as well as dynamic loading and unloading, the algorithm animation environment does not have to be exited.

Because the notion of parameters to algorithms, input generators, and views is rather unconventional, we now elaborate.

Algorithms, input generators, and views can all be tuned directly by the end-user. Just what the parameters mean for any particular algorithm, input generator, or view depends on how it was implemented. Thus, it is the programmer, not the end-user, who decides what the parameters are—whether the particular component will even have any parameters, what the user interface will be that controls how they are set, what their default values are, and so forth. The user interface management tools and guidelines of the underlying workstation environment promote consistency in the user interface for manipulating parameters across many domains.

Algorithm parameters affect the algorithm, not the data that the algorithm manipulates. For example, should the lexical analyzer in an animated compiler use a hash table of size 119 or 2001? Or should it use a binary tree (or some specific type of balanced tree) rather than a hash table? *Input parameters* affect the input generators. For example, the input parameter to a generator that reads numbers from a file for sorting algorithms would be the name of the file. Another generator for the same sorting algorithm might produce random numbers; the parameters for this generator would be how many numbers to produce and a seed for a random number generator. Of course, an input parameter will affect the data indirectly, which in turn will affect the algorithm. *View parameters* affect how information is displayed in a particular view window; they do not affect the algorithm or input generator. For example, should a node in a graph be displayed as a circle or as a square? Should text inside the node scale with the size of the node, or stay a fixed size? The end-user's display preferences are not relevant to the algorithm or to the input generator.

Using parameters to interact with programs is a novel approach. It provides a consistent framework for allowing end-users to specify various types of information when they want, not when the program wants it. In general, algorithm and input generator parameters are specified before an algorithm runs; view parameters can be changed while a program is running or even after it has finished. At any time, the end-user can observe the current values of any of the parameters. Unfortunately, this strategy does not work 100% of the time. There are situations in which information cannot be specified before a program runs—for example, picking a node to delete in a binary tree—because they are based to some extent on the current runtime state of the algorithm. Such information is called *runtime-specifics*.

Programmer's Model

While algorithms, input generators, and views are highly interrelated, they must also be independent and must conform to rigid interface specifications in order to work with one another and with the algorithm animation system. Each algorithm has two parts: code to implement the algorithm and code to manipulate end-user parameters. Similarly, each input generator and each view has a separate part to handle its end-user parameters. As will be described in later chapters, each component has additional parts to handle other specific functions. An overview of the relationship among components is shown in Figure 1.2.

Algorithms are coded in a high-level language such as PASCAL and are annotated with markers called *interesting events* or *algorithm events*, indicating the phenomena that will be of interest when the program runs. One type of algorithm event, an *output event*, corresponds to the points at which a *Writeln* might have been placed for debugging, tracing or generating output of the algorithm in a non-graphical environment. When the program runs within the algorithm animation environment, all views on the screen are notified whenever an output event occurs and each view updates itself as appropriate to reflect the event. The other type of algorithm event, an *input event*, corresponds to the place at which a *Readln* might have appeared in

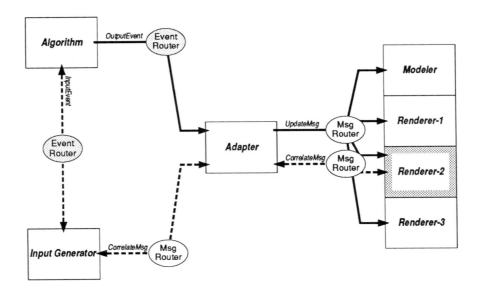

Figure 1.2: *Relationship among components that a client-programmer implements to animate algorithms. Boxes represent components implemented by the programmer, and ovals represent parts of the algorithm animation system that are responsible for routing information among components. Solid arrows indicate unidirectional flow of information, and dashed arrows indicate bidirectional flow. The renderer associated with the view window having the keyboard focus is highlighted.*

a conventional implementation of the algorithm. During execution, the current input generator is notified of each input event and responds by returning some data to the algorithm.

Events are an important aspect of the conceptual model. Essentially, an event is a "code atom" which serves the following purposes: (1) it gives a name to a segment of code so end-users can refer to it; (2) the end-user can associate a cost to computing the segment; (3) the end-user can single-step and set breakpoints based on events; and finally (4a) an output event is a signal for the views to update themselves and (4b) an input event is a signal for the input generator to provide the algorithm with data.

Algorithm events are the software analogue of an oscilloscope: the output events correspond to points on a circuit where the probe leads are attached to observe signals of interest, and input events correspond to connecting a circuit's input port to power, ground, or some other circuit. The end-user is aware of events because they provide the abstraction through which the algorithm's execution is controlled.

A view embodies a synthetic, dynamic, graphical entity. The image displayed on the screen is the result of *update messages* the view receives; a view does not access an algorithm's data structures. A view is internally structured into a *modeler* and a *renderer*: the modeler maintains the model which the renderer displays on the screen in a view window. Multiple renderers can be simultaneously displaying (in different ways) the same model (in separate windows). An *adapter* converts algorithm output events into update messages understood by the modelers and renderers. Consequently, views can be used without change in a variety of algorithms; in addition, as we shall see, views can be chained together to display aspects of themselves.

Views can also be used to allow the end-user to provide input graphically in response to an algorithm input event by pointing in a view window. Because only the renderer knows how the model is displayed on the screen, the input generator must query the renderer to correlate a point on the screen to the model. The adapter is also used to convert the queries and responses between the input generator and the renderer associated with the view window that has the current keyboard focus; the queries are called *correlate messages*. Syntactic error-checking can be done in the renderer, but semantic checking must be done either by the input generator or the algorithm. Specifying information graphically is not always meaningful in all views.

Cast of Characters

Algorithm animation involves a variety of activities, each of which draws on the skills of a particular group of people. Because a primary focus of this thesis is to consider just what tools are needed to animate programs, we first need to identify this cast of characters. These classifications are just for the sake of analysis; a single person often plays multiple roles.

The *end-users* actually use the environment interactively to explore algorithms in action. They use a specialized interpreter to control the execution of the available algorithms, and a specialized user interface to manipulate windows in which to view the execution via any of the available graphical displays. They can run the algorithms using a wide assortment of input generators and various instantiations of any particular input generator. Because there are many possible ways to connect algorithms, views, and inputs, end-users can generate displays never seen by the client-programmers who implemented the pieces.

End-users are called *script authors* and *script readers* when they use the system as an electronic medium for communication by creating and replaying scripts. In an educational setting, the script authors are often the instructors and the readers are the students. Often, a person coding a new algorithm or view will also prepare a script to illustrate properties of the algorithm or view. When an end-user is devising a new script or browsing through an existing script, there are additional commands that are not normally available, e.g., commands that control what type of information is saved or restored, command that traverse the dynamic document, and so on.

There are two types of client-programmers. The first type, *algorithmaticians*, take the actual algorithms being animated, often from a textbook, journal paper, or even existing applications, and augment them with markers indicating interesting phenomena that should give rise to some type of display. The algorithmaticians usually also implement the input generators and the adapters. In an educational setting, the course instructor and teaching assistants are usually the algorithmaticians. In a research environment, the researchers themselves are usually the algorithmaticians. This process must require only a nominal amount of effort in order for an algorithm animation system to be successful.

The second type of client-programmer, *animators*, design and implement the view code which actually displays algorithms in execution, i.e., renderers and modelers. They code in a high-level language, such as PASCAL or C, and use a library of graphical primitives provided through the algorithm animation system. Ideally, these people should have training in graphic design; in reality, however, these people are usually computer scientists without formal artistic training. They should have access to graphic designers with whom effective displays can be jointly developed. Achieving real-time animation often requires low-level system-dependent coding.

The central figure in any software environment is the *systems guru*, the person responsible for implementing, maintaining, enhancing and debugging the system. Systems gurus must be very competent systems programmers; they serve as the interface between the people who use the system interactively (end-users in general, and script authors and script readers in particular) and those who use the algorithm animation system as programmers (algorithmaticians and animators). As an algorithm animation system matures, the need for a systems guru diminishes.

1.4 Perspective on Graphics in Programming

Algorithm animation is a form of *program visualization*, "the use of the technology of interactive graphics and the crafts of graphic design, typography, animation, and cinematography to enhance the presentation and understanding of computer programs. Program visualization is related to but distinct from the discipline of *visual programming* which is the use of various two-dimensional or diagrammatic notations in the programming process" [8]. Visual programming also includes those programming-by-example, by-demonstration or by-constraints systems that use graphical objects as fundamental computational entities. A number of surveys about visual programming have appeared recently [20, 21, 32, 55]. Displays of the execution of visual languages used in visual programming can be easily confused with program visualization. More to the point, they *should* be entirely similar! Systems such as GARDEN [58] strive to unify these two disciplines; that approach, however, is not our concern here.

Program visualization systems can be classified by whether they illustrate code or data, and whether displays are dynamic or static [53]. In addition, dynamic displays are either interactive or passive, such as a videotape. Algorithm animation displays are dynamic displays showing a program's fundamental *operations*; operations embody both transformations and accesses to data and to a lesser extent, flow-of-control.

Typical static displays of program code are flowcharts, Nassi-Shneiderman diagrams, scoping diagrams, and module interconnections, as well as text itself when enhanced through formatting and typography. Numerous systems have been developed to display one or more such diagrams automatically from programs coded in high-level procedural languages, and to use the diagrams for editing the underlying program. Static displays of program structure can be animated automatically by highlighting the appropriate parts as the code runs.

Static displays of program data are more difficult to create automatically than static displays of code. One problem is that a given data structure can be implemented in many different ways, and a second problem is that a data structure has many different representations. Typically the more informative displays are not the canonical displays that can be created automatically, but are those discovered only through experimentation. Even canonical displays are difficult to construct for arbitrarily linked structures; they tend to look like rat's nests and lose meaning. This thesis presents no new layout algorithms for static displays of data structures. We assume that either such a package is available (Chapter 2 cites some packages) or the user is interested in a customized display to illustrate particular features of an algorithm.

Creating dynamic displays of program data has all of the problems that creating static displays has and more. In particular, dynamic displays must decide when the display should be updated and how this should be done incrementally to look effective. The precise definition of what constitutes an "effective" display is beyond our scope here. It is subjective, and involves many complex, interacting and competing factors, such as the viewer's visual vocabulary, the speed of the changes, the techniques used for highlighting, and so on.

Algorithm animation displays can be thought of a dynamic displays of an algorithm's operations, not merely its data or structure. We now explore the nature of these displays in depth.

Algorithm Animation Displays

Algorithm animation displays can be described using three dimensions, as shown in Figure 1.3. The *content* of the displays ranges from direct representations of the program's data to synthetic images information not necessarily inside the program. The *persistence* dimension ranges from displays that show only the current state of information to those that show a complete history of each change in the information. The *transformation* dimension ranges from displays that show changes in the pictures discretely to those that show incremental and continuous changes.

Readers are encouraged to pause at this point to scan through the screen images in Chapter 3. We will refer to those images in the remainder of this section to illustrate the various types of algorithm animation displays. In addition, Figures 1.4 and 1.5 show typical displays in the BALSA–I algorithm animation environment. Figure 1.4 shown First-Fit Binpacking operating on

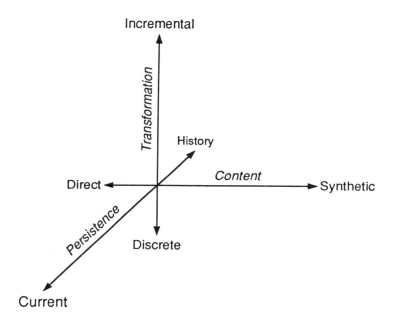

Figure 1.3: *Attributes of dynamic algorithm animation displays along three axes. Displays classified in the rear upper right corner (synthetic, history, and incremental) are usually the most intricate to implement, and those in the front lower left (direct, current, and discrete) the easiest.*

a relatively small amount of data; Figure 1.5 shows four different binpacking algorithms operating on a much larger amount of data.

First, we will look at the content axis. *Direct* displays are pictures that are isomorphic to one or more data structures in the program. At a given instant, the data structure(s) could be constructed from the display, and the display could be constructed from the data structure(s). No additional information is needed. For example, the Bins view (Figure 1.4) in a direct view of the array *bins*. The Dots view (Figure 3.3) is a direct view of the array of numbers being sorted.

Synthetic displays, on the other hand, do not have a mapping to any program variables. They can show the operations causing changes in the data, or can be abstractions of the data. The Waste view (Figures 1.4 and 1.5)

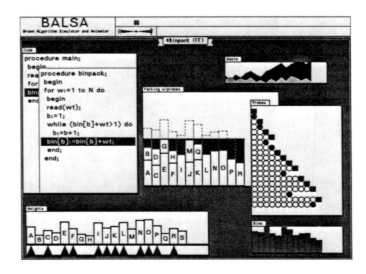

Figure 1.4: *First-fit binpacking algorithm.*

is a good example of a synthetic view: after each weight is inserted in the bin, the graphs are continued at the right edge to show how much space is wasted. The top graph shows the wasted space and the bottom graph shows the lower bound of this quantity. The concept of wasted space is not in the program. The Probes view (Figure 1.4) is also a synthetic view. Each row corresponds to searching for a bin in which to insert a new weight. A hollow icon indicates a bin did not have enough room for the weight, whereas a filled icon indicates that it did. A square icon indicates that the weight is the first one in a bin; the circle indicates a bin that has been started already.

Many displays are composites of direct and synthetic components. For example, the Compare-Exchange view (Figure 3.1) shows some values of the array; additional information (showing the results of comparisons or exchanges) is encoded as the color of the elements. A proper reading of the picture would enable the current contents of the array to be reconstructed, although this property is not invertible: the picture could not be reconstructed just by knowing the contents of the array at an instant of time. This view shows more than simply changes to the algorithms data structure; it shows both the fundamental operations the algorithm performs, and the

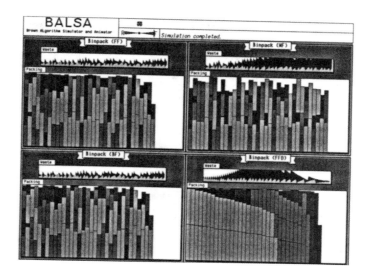

Figure 1.5: *Four binpacking algorithms.*

flow of control: each iteration of the algorithm's main loop is displayed on a separate line.

A second criterion for classifying displays is whether a display shows *current* information or illustrates a *history* of what has happened. In Figure 1.4, all views except for the Bins view shows some history. The **Weights** view is a history of each weight inserted into a bin, the variable *wt*. A triangle is drawn beneath a weight when that weight causes a new bin to be started; thus, it is a history of a synthetic entity. In the **Waste** view, only the right edge shows the current waste; the part of the graph leading up to the right edge is a history of the waste as each weight is processed. The **Probes** view shows a history of each and every bin that was tested to see whether or not it could support the new weight. Even the **Code** view shows history!

The third and final criterion by which we can classify animations is based on the nature of the transitions from the old displays to the new ones. *Incremental* transformations show a smooth transition. For example, in the **Packing w/probes** view in Figure 1.4, the dotted box showing the attempt to put a new weight into each of the bins, advances smoothly from one bin to the next, while also keeping a trace of itself. *Discrete* transitions are just that: the old value is erased and the new value is drawn. All of the views in Figure 1.4, with the above mentioned exception, are discrete transitions.

Discrete transformations are perceived as incremental when the difference between the new and old pictures is "small enough" in relationship to the complexity of the data. Genuinely discrete transformations tend to be most useful on large sets of data. Incremental transitions are most effective when users are examining an algorithm running on a small set of data; in fact, incremental transformations tend to hinder the display of large data because they slow down the animation significantly and contain too much low-level detail. Unless a good animation package is provided, incremental transitions are often tedious and difficult to program.

Another issue that incremental transformations must address is how much time they should consume. For example, changing a single pointer in a tree might cause a very large subtree to move a large distance (which might also necessitate repositioning all nodes in the tree). How fast should the subtree movement be? Should it be at the same speed as if it moved a small amount? Or should the total movement consume a constant amount of time, so that it moves quickly if it has a large distance to cover?

1.5 Automatic Algorithm Animations

What is it about algorithm animation that is more than simply monitoring a variable? That is, why could we not simply associate a procedure with a variable that would be called each time the variable is modified or accessed, with information about which part of it was modified or accessed? In particular, annotating the algorithm with interesting event markers and creating the specialized displays are time-consuming and error-prone activities. Can these activities be automated or eliminated?

Algorithm animation displays cannot be created automatically because they are essentially monitors of the algorithm's fundamental *operations*; an algorithm's operations cannot be deduced from an arbitrary algorithm automatically but must be denoted by a person with knowledge of the operations performed by the algorithm. In addition, there are problems relating to real-time *performance* and to *informative displays*. We shall return to these problems below.

Even if we assume that an algorithm's operations have been identified, automatically creating pictures to depict the operations is not currently feasible. Although graphic designers have worked on a semiology of display techniques for static information [12, 13, 67], except in a few highly specialized application domains, they have not had the tools to create dynamic displays and therefore have not looked at the issues involved in their semiology. Moreover, many data structures and algorithms are highly specialized and require one-of-a-kind displays to make aspects of their properties understandable. Some knowledge-based systems have been built that present meaningful pictures and even animations, but in restricted domains [25, 48]. More experience is needed with animated algorithm displays before we can hope to automate the task, though libraries of standard displays are possible.

Automatic Program Visualization Displays

We now examine in more detail the nature of program visualization displays that can be created automatically. Dynamic displays require two types of information: the *entity* to be displayed and a *delta* describing the change in the entity. Static displays need only information regarding the entity.

Dynamic and static displays of static or even executing code or program structures can be created automatically because the set of entities and deltas is well-defined and can be accessed directly by a display routine. The entities are derived from the source code, and the deltas from the changes in the program counter. Examples of code entities are procedures, statements, files, and blocks; examples of deltas are advancing to the next line of code, entering or exiting a procedure, and entering or exiting a block.

Dynamic and static displays of data can also be created automatically. The entities are the data structure(s) to be displayed, and the deltas can be inferred by examining the data each time it is accessed or modified. A routine to display a static picture of the data structure automatically would access the data through the runtime environment. It would need to be told how the data is represented in the program (i.e., a mapping into a canonical representation) and what type of display is desired (i.e., a display technique for the canonical representation). Although canonical displays can be created without modifying the algorithm, they are not always very informative, especially for non-trivial data structures.

Moreover, dynamic displays created automatically do not show the delta in the way the change is conceptualized. This problem is because only the "before" and "after" conditions of the data are known and the display can do nothing more than interpolate between the two states. Consequently, views that are direct views of data structures and are updated discretely can be created automatically, subject to the inherent problems with displaying data mentioned above, because they do not attempt to display the deltas.

Difficulties of Algorithm Animation Displays

We now examine in detail the problems with creating algorithm animation displays automatically.

Problem 1. Capturing operations. Algorithm operations do not necessarily correspond to each access or modification of the algorithm's data structures. In particular, (a) accessing a particular variable has different meanings at different locations in the algorithm, and (b) an arbitrary number of accesses and modifications (including zero) results in a single operation.

The following fragment of Quicksort illustrates the first of these problems:

```
      ...
      if r − l ≤ M then
        for i := 2 to N do
          begin
          v := a[i]; j := i;
          while a[j − 1] > v do
            begin a[j] := a[j − 1]; j := j − 1; end;
          a[j] := v
          end
      else
        begin
        v := a[r]; i := l − 1; j := r;
        repeat
          repeat i := i + 1 until a[i] ≥ v;
          repeat j := j − 1 until a[j] ≤ v;
          t := a[i]; a[i] := a[j]; a[j] := t;
        until j ≤ i;
        a[j] := a[i]; a[i] := a[r]; a[r] := t
        end
      ...
```

If the subfile being sorted (the elements between l and r) is small enough, Insertion sort is used to sort the subfile. Two fundamental operations are being performed on the array: "set value" (in the **then** part) and "exchange" (in the **else** part). A client-programmer would like to illustrate these operations differently.

A monitor cannot not know which accesses to array a constitute a "set value," and which an "exchange." Even if this problem were eliminated, say by re-coding the Insertion sort phase using exchanges, a second, more difficult, problem remains: how can a monitor infer which accesses comprise an exchange? It is the result of a variable number of modifications to the array; it is not the result of every other modification. Of course, one could always change the Quicksort code fragment to guarantee that every exchange is the result of exactly two modifications. We assert, however, that to do so would be just as difficult and error-prone—if not more so—than adding the algorithm event annotations that our model requires. Moreover, it would be counter to one of our primary goals: minimal intrusions into the original algorithm's original source code.

The second aspect of the problem, that of an arbitrary number of accesses and modifications resulting in a single operation, is seen in the **Partition-Tree** view in Figure 3.5. The shape of the tree is determined by the algorithm operation, "ElementInPlace." To simplify the discussion, assume that Insertion sort is not used for the small subfiies. That is, remove all code in Quicksort fragment above except the body of the **else** statement. After the modified fragment has been executed, the value stored in a[i] is finalized. This abstract operation cannot be inferred by simply monitoring variables: it is a conceptual operation that is essentially triggered by the control flow.

Another example of this second aspect of the problem is illustrated in the following fragment of code from an implementation of Pairing Heaps [29] (the pairing heap is stored using right-sibling and left-child links, with back pointers to each node's parent):

```
...
back[0] := 0;
if (info[x] < info[y])
  then begin rbro[x] := rbro[y]; back[rbro[y]] := x; end
  else begin
    back[y] := back[x];
    if (rbro[back[x]] = x)
      then rbro[back[x]] := y
      else lson[back[x]] := y;
    t := x; x := y; y := t;
  end;
rbro[y] := lson[x]; back[lson[x]] := y;
lson[x] := y; back[y] := x;
...
```

This rather complex sequence of pointer manipulations performs a single (and rather simple) "link" operation of subtrees x and y. Linking two subtrees involves making the subtree with the larger root node the leftmost son of the other subtree. A monitor would need to coordinate accesses and modifications to four arrays (*info*, *back*, *rbro*, and *lson*). Note that displaying the data at each operation would result in pictures that are misleading and would obscure the essence of the link operation.

Problem 2. Real-time performance. In general, the data being accessed or modified may be costly to identify, resulting in unacceptable performance. For example, knowing which node in a tree is being modified may lead to costly computation to determine its parent, siblings, and children. Just because a task is expensive does not mean that it is impossible; however, for the real-time interactive systems that we address in this thesis, performance is a real issue. One cannot just hope for faster hardware or clever display algorithms, since for every increase in hardware or algorithm speed, the complexity of the algorithms and the size of the data that one will wish to animate is bound to also increase.

Problem 3. Informative displays. Many displays necessitate detailed knowledge about the algorithm's runtime behavior and the specific data upon which the algorithm will be run. In fact, the optimal size and layout parameters for some displays require two passes. For example, because the Partition-Tree view knows that the height of the tree will be about equal to the binary logarithm of the number of elements in the corresponding array, it can allocate that much vertical space from the start. However, it cannot know the exact height until the algorithm runs.

Towards Automatic Algorithm Animation Displays

Algorithm operations must be identified by a programmer. Languages that support abstract data types are particularly well-suited to this approach. For example, in Smalltalk, entities and their deltas are defined by objects and the messages they react to. Given a properly modularized Smalltalk program, one just needs to specify how the objects and messages map into entities and deltas. This approach is not limited to Smalltalk, object-oriented programming languages, or data abstraction languages. In conventional programming languages, such as PASCAL or C, one could encapsulate the operations in procedure calls (there would be a one-to-one mapping between the procedure calls and the Smalltalk messages), which could then be monitored automatically.

It is tempting to believe that such a strategy is a panacea. However, algorithms from textbooks and journals are given in "straight-line" code; they are not broken into procedures. It is impossible to take straight-line code and to infer automatically the correct abstractions to form the encapsulations.

Consider, for instance, the fragment of Quicksort from above. After the algorithm operations have been encapsulated (by hand) into procedure calls, it becomes:

```
...
repeat
   repeat i := i + 1; until Compare(a[i], v, '≥');
   repeat j := j − 1; until Compare(a[j], v, '≤');
   Exchange(a[i], a[j]);
until j ≤ i;
Exchange(a[i], a[j]); Exchange(a[i], a[r]);
ElementInPlace(i);
...
```

The procedure *ElementInPlace* does nothing; it has been added strictly for animation purposes. The difficult issue of annotating an algorithm is one of identifying the phenomena of interest in the program; the appropriate syntax for enunciating the abstractions may or may not be directly supported in the implementation language.

The approach we have taken in BALSA–I and BALSA–II is to annotate algorithms with "events" rather than forcing the algorithmatician to radically proceduralize his algorithm to encapsulate each meaningful operation. This approach minimizes the changes to the algorithm, since the algorithm is augmented, not transformed. Of course, if an algorithmatician is willing to procedurize the algorithm, events can be inferred "automatically" by a rather simple preprocessor that inserts an annotation as the first statement of each procedure. The parameters of the event would be the name of the procedure, followed by the arguments of the procedure.

Events also help to solve the second and third problems mentioned above. Data that may be costly to identify automatically can often be identified by the algorithm and associated with the event. Other events can broadcast information of interest concerning the characteristics of the algorithms; displays can adjust parameters appropriately.

There are numerous additional pleasant side-effects of having annotations in the algorithm which we shall discuss briefly here and explore more fully in later chapters. The end-user can specify events for setting breakpoints, setting granularity of single stepping, and marking how much time each event should take to execute. The animator can debug a view independent of the algorithm, by feeding it a stream of events generated by hand (or even randomly). The algorithm need not be implemented in any specific language as long as it is callable by the algorithm animation system, nor are there any restrictions on the data structures used in the algorithm. The systems guru can give the end-user the illusion of an interpreter—one that is language-independent! Annotations give flow of control back to the algorithm animation system, which can then poll the end-user to see whether execution should be paused.

1.6 Disclaimers

This thesis does not address the issue of what makes for the most effective displays of operations, data, or code; we have noted some preliminary observations elsewhere [18]. Fortunately, the pictures that concern us do not need to be realistic images. They can have "jaggies" and do not need texture, shadows, reflections, or refractions. They exist to communicate information, not as objects of art—although many images, especially those involving color, are quite attractive. In fact, it is unlikely that one could ever claim that one particular display is the best. Each display highlights particular features of the program, and thus is more or less desirable depending on its intended use. Moreover, a given picture can mean several different things to each viewer, and the meaning will change depending on many factors, such as what other images are simultaneously begin displayed, how developed one's "visual vocabulary" is, and so on. Consequently, an algorithm animation system should not impose a rigid set of displays for programs; rather, it should make it easy to create new displays and use existing displays to explore the runtime nature of a wide variety of programs.

Another aspect we do not address here is how fast the animation should take place, or with what granularity. It is essential, however, that an algorithm animation system allow users to control the speed. Not surprisingly, it has been shown that information is lost if an animation is either too fast or too slow [49]. The optimum speed depends on the viewer and the purpose of the animation. In practice, we have found that, as one would expect, viewers can get a high-level intuition for the dynamics of an algorithm when relatively fast speeds are used. To understand details of the behavior, however, relatively slow speeds are required. The absolute speed also depends on the complete ensemble of views on the screen; complex views or multiple views often require slower speeds to let the user digest all of the information on the screen. Displays showing representations that are unfamiliar to viewers also require slow speeds—at least until the displays are incorporated into the viewer's visual vocabulary.

Our environment for algorithm animation is oriented to sequential programming in the small. It has been tuned for "algorithms" such as those found in a typical textbook or journal article. These are usually less than a page or two of high-level procedural code, and are self-contained with simplified data assumptions. For example, a priority queue "algorithm" might operate on small integers, whereas in practice the priority queue "program" might be embedded in a database system and would operate on names and manufacturers of automobiles. "Programming in the small" does not, by any means, imply trivial or toy programs. Experience has shown that relatively little is understood mathematically or otherwise about many small (in size), well-known, fundamental algorithms. There is a huge world of small programs to be explored, many of which form the basis of large real-world systems. While many aspects of an algorithm animation environment scale to large systems, however, programming in the large needs additional tools that are beyond the scope of this research.

1.7 Thesis Outline

In the next chapter, we review previous work on animation of programs. We limit ourselves to displays of data, not program structure or code, both static and dynamic. This chapter provides background reading and is self-contained. In Chapter 3, we present a tour through the interactive environment of our prototype system, BALSA–II. Here we discuss not how one goes about animating a program, but rather how one uses the environment for exploring algorithms. We also present a formal description of the interactive environment. If you read only one chapter, read this one. If you read more than one other chapter, also read this one; the remaining chapters assume familiarity with the interactive nature of the prototype. Chapter 4 discusses using the interactive environment for creating dynamic documents. It describes our model of dynamic documents and the user interface presented to script writers and script readers, and discusses various implementation aspects.

In Chapter 5, we leave the realm of the end-user and enter that of the programmer. We present in detail our model of how client-programmers go about animating their algorithms, implementing the necessary input generators, and building graphical displays. In Chapter 6, we present an overview of how BALSA–II is implemented. The system is the glue that binds the algorithms, input generators, and views, to the end-users, script writers, and script viewers. We conclude in Chapter 7 with a discussion of areas for future research, both short-term and long-term.

2

Related Work

This chapter reviews previous and current work that has directly influenced and been influenced by our research. We have intentionally ignored the plethora of special-purpose, primarily educational systems because, by and large, they are hard-wired for one or more particular algorithms. A very impressive system of this genre is Andromeda's "Visible Compilers" for simplified dialects of Algol and Ada [4]. We also do not review the literature relating to process or program monitoring (see [27] and [54] respectively for good surveys), as well as those systems we classified in Chapter 1 as "visual programming" or those displaying program structure [20, 21, 32, 55].

Three types of work have influenced the present research: movies of algorithms in action, debuggers displaying data structures graphically, and algorithm animation systems. We discuss each of these in turn. We also evaluate our preliminary work in BALSA–I in detail, trace the various systems that influenced that effort, and discuss the systems that it has inspired. As before, we will use "BALSA–I" and "BALSA–II" when specific aspects of those systems are important; when facets of both systems are similar, we will just use "BALSA."

2.1 Algorithm Movies

From the start of the "computer graphics" era in the early '60s through the end of the '70s, graphics hardware was a scarce and expensive commodity. While the opportunity to use the hardware was small, its potential—especially for educators—was great.

The obvious solution to this problem in the mid–'70s was to record the computer-generated images on film, "[since] the cost of on-line computer use is, of course, much higher than the print cost of a film" [37]. A more outspoken variation on this theme had been presented by Huggins and Entwisle a few years earlier [39]:

> We consider the notion that [animated computer graphics] ... should be produced individually under the interactive control of a single student for his sole benefit to be an economic absurdity at present ... Hence, to those wealthy few, who are fortunate to have such graphical displays available, we direct a plea that they should consider arrangements by which other interested members of the academic community can use their facilities for the very beneficial production of computer-animated films for the entire community.

The basic limitation of films is, of course, that they do not allow viewers to experiment with the model being displayed. Viewers must watch the film in the exact form in which it was produced, with the exact parameters, the exact data and, almost always, even at the exact speed. Despite these inherent limitations, however, films are better than nothing and quite a few pedagogical computer-animated films were made in the '60s and '70s. Interestingly enough, only a handful of them were on computer science topics, as opposed to, say, physics, chemistry, or mathematics. Huggins, in his landmark paper on iconic communication [38], goes one step further to claim that any computer scientist's film will be poor:

> ...I must conclude it is unfortunate that present development of computer-graphic facilities for purpose of iconic communication ... rests largely in the hands of computer science specialists because I find that the skills for visual expression seem to be curiously lacking among practitioners of that discipline.

The remainder of this section describes four important computer-animated films of computers in action. Undoubtedly, films and videotapes have been made of working sessions of virtually every system cited in this thesis; we consider those "systems" rather than "films" since it is the systems aspects of those projects that are of interest.

The first computer-generated movie concerning computers was produced by Knowlton at Bell Labs in 1966. The movie, *L6: Bell Telephone Laboratories Low-Level Linked List Language* [42], portrayed the workings of an assembly-level list-processing language. A memorable aspect of the film were the "bugs" that crawled along linked lists.

Hopgood's movie on hashing algorithms [37] in 1974 was the first movie whose ostensible purpose was to portray an algorithm. The movie contained three synthetic views, updated discretely. The views were of: a hash table where each entry showed not only whether or not the slot was taken, but also how many collisions were encountered when the element was inserted; a graph of the number of probes needed to insert each item; and the value of the maximum number of collisions to insert any item. A significant contribution of this movie was that it showed a data structure in a state that was too large to have been computed by hand-simulation. The movie also displayed the effects of altering parameters to the algorithm (e.g., the size of the hash table), as well as how the algorithm performed with different types of input.

Booth's *PQ-Trees* [14], produced the following year, showed the effect of various algorithms on a PQ-tree data structure. The tree was displayed as a stick figure, with nodes and branches highlighted in one of three colors. When the data structure changed, the movie showed a smooth, incremental animation of the way it was transformed. Techniques included simultaneously rotating subtrees, raising and lowering subtrees, and changing node shapes.

Baecker's stellar *Sorting Out Sorting* [9], first shown at SIGGRAPH '81, illustrated a number of different sorting algorithms running on both small and large data sets. The small data sets were usually represented by sticks of various heights, while the large data sets were portrayed using the endpoints of the sticks, forming a distinctively shaped "cloud of dots." Baecker used a small set of colors for highlighting. The movie also contained a sound track, although merely a narrative one—sound was not used to give more insight into the workings of the algorithms. The movie showed algorithm races, as well as reverse execution. Unfortunately, while it was undoubtedly the pinnacle of algorithm movies, both technically and aesthetically, it also required an extremely large amount of time and effort to produce: the 30-minute film was three years in the making!

With the advent of affordable graphics-based workstations, interactive systems have replaced movies for most applications. Now, computer time is cheap—free, in most cases—whereas film is cumbersome and the equipment required to make good-quality films is relatively expensive. Most importantly, interactive systems are superior to passive movies. But interactive systems raise a new set of issues concerning user interactions that do not exist with movies.

2.2 Graphical Display of Data Structures

A number of systems have been built that automatically produce a static
graphical display of a program's data structures from the information available to the system debugger at runtime. These systems have the advantage
that data structures in any arbitrary program can be viewed without altering
the program in any way, but the disadvantage that the generic representation
does not necessarily convey how the data is really used. A data structure
is more than just the replication of its individual elements; the interrela-
tionships among data elements is often an essential aspect. Moreover, as
discussed in Chapter 1, a static display, albeit graphical, does not reveal
how the algorithm is processing the data, nor does updating the display in
response to each change in the data.

Displaying data structures for debugging has different constraints from
creating views for algorithm animation. For debugging, the displays must
be extraordinarily robust (after all, one of their primary purposes is to reveal incorrect data), and consequently they are more complex to implement
than displays oriented to algorithm animation. Another problem unique to
displays for debugging is that of naming: every data structure must identify itself as well as each of its components. In algorithm animation, as
mentioned in Chapter 1, simplifications can be made to the data format.

Numerous layout algorithms have been proposed for canonical displays
of trees [56, 71], and recently for graphs [46]. A general-purpose package,
GELO allows a programmer to describe a layout of linked hierarchical objects
through constraints [59]; it is part of Reiss's GARDEN graphical programming environment cited earlier. Unfortunately, no work has apparently been
done on applying principles of graphic design to drawing even static pictures
of data structures.

Incense

Incense [52, 51] was implemented by Myers at Xerox PARC in the late '70s
in conjunction with the strongly typed Mesa programming environment.
When the user specified the name of variable in the program being executed,
the system would generate a graphical display of that data structure in a
user-specified rectangular region on the screen. Associated with each data
type was one or more *formats* for presenting different pictures of the data

structure. In the final version of the system, however, only a default format was supported.

Briefly, the process for displaying a data structure was as follows. An *artist*, part of a format, was invoked with parameters specifying the location on the screen in which to draw the data. The data values were then found using the Mesa runtime tables, and the artist would either display something (textually, iconically, or invisibly—depending on the amount of screen space) or (if it was a record or an array) cause the system to invoke the appropriate artists associated with each of the components, after deciding how much space to allocate to each. If the data type to be displayed contained pointer(s), a *layout*, also part of a format, was invoked to divide the bounding rectangle into regions for the node and each referent. When the artist was eventually invoked to display a pointer, the artist first caused the system to ensure that the referent was displayed. Thus, recursively defined structures would be displayed with increasingly smaller-sized children. Consequently, arbitrarily complex data was guaranteed always to fit into any specified rectangular region.

Incense never was used in production. One problem was efficiency: displaying a binary tree consisting of eight nodes on six levels required 33 seconds on the existing hardware (a 128KB Xerox Alto). Also, the system was never integrated in the standard system debugger, which severely limited its usefulness. As a vehicle for viewing program data, it did not support user-defined displays, although it had been planned to add that feature.

PV

The PV project at CCA [15, 35, 44] was an ambitious attempt to use graphics in all phases of programming large systems (ca., 10^6 lines of code). Displaying data structures was just one of the phases; other phases concentrated on displays of the program structure. "The PV system will, in effect, 'open the side of the machine' to permit users to look inside and watch their programs run" [35]. Unfortunately, funding for the project was cut just as the implementation of the prototype was beginning, and consequently much of the literature only reports in the abstract on what a PV system should support, what a typical screen might look like, how a user might specify such and such, and so on. The details of how to do these things are addressed but superficially.

The PV prototype system was implemented on a UNIX-based mainframe, with multiple color monitors. It was felt that multiple windows on a single monitor did not provide enough screen real estate for the large programs they planned to display. PV took completely unmodified code and compiled it with appropriate hooks that enabled the system to get control each time a variable was modified [44], in much the same way as conventional debuggers work.

Two types of animations of data were supported: in-place updates of values, and indicators moving along horizontal or vertical scales that could be used to depict arrays and their indices. It was claimed that PV also supported "creation, rearrangement, and deletion of data cells to reflect altered pointer assignments," but no basis for this claims appears in the rest of the paper [15]. A contribution of this project was the way in which the user could "bind" an animation to the source code: at runtime, the end-user selected the desired type of animation and specified the names of the variables corresponding to the static graphical components of the dynamic visualization. This strategy is possible because the types of displays are very limited, and because the displays were direct views of program variables.

GDBX

Another system that provided graphical displays of arbitrary data structures for debugging was Baskerville's GDBX [10]. GDBX, integrated with the standard UNIX debugger, DBX, ran on a Sun Microsystems workstation. The system was designed to be a production-quality tool; as such, it eliminated some of the generality envisioned in Incense, such as user-defined displays. The most obvious way in which it differed from Incense was in its algorithm for displaying linked structures on the screen.

GDBX displayed a record in nested-box notation: a box was tiled with its various components. For dynamic data, the end-user could specify whether the links should grow horizontally (to the right) or vertically (down); unlike Incense, all nodes of a given record were displayed in the same size. That is, nodes did not shrink when they were children. Data structures were displayed in a standard Sun window whose contents could be scrolled horizontally and vertically if the data structure exceeded the window real estate. The end-user could force the display of a data structure to become larger or smaller by changing the font used to label the components of a record, and could also control which fields of which data structures to display, as well as how far to chase a particular pointer field.

Unlike Incense, GDBX supported a limited form of editing the data via the view. The user could pick up a pointer field and drag it to any node on the screen. This change was reflected in the contents of the pointer field as well as on the screen. GDBX also animated variables by redisplaying the changed fields of the specified data structure without first erasing them after each step in the debugger. Modified fields were highlighted by blinking.

The primary shortcoming of GDBX was its generic and rudimentary display of the data. No provisions were made for user-defined displays. Also, as a graphical display of data structure, it only monitored data. Interesting displays, especially those that reflect interrelations among variables, could not be supported.

PROVIDE

Moher's PROVIDE [50], developed at the University of Illinois at Chicago, used multiple Macintoshes as a graphical front end to a VAX 11/780. The program being animated was compiled on the mainframe and run there, and an extensive execution trace was stored on disk. The user could then observe the execution through the Macs, and control what part of the program's execution to view by making queries of the database.

As in PV, the end-user decided at runtime which program variables to bind to virtual parameters that drove graphical images. As an example, consider three quantities A, B, and C which are to be displayed as a pie chart with three wedges. At runtime, the end-user could specify which program variables corresponded to A, B, and C, and could also specify labels for the entire chart and for each of the wedges. In general, one variable could drive several pictures, and a given picture could be driven by more than one variable. PROVIDE allowed the end-user to group one or more contiguous statements into an atomic unit, and only after the atomic unit was executed would the picture be notified that it must be redisplayed. This eliminated the problem of displaying inconsistent pictures while a data structure was being modified.

PROVIDE, like GDBX, had a notion of "graphical editing." Upon user request, a picture would display its *editing handles*. For example, the editing handles for a histogram corresponding an array of integers were little knobs at the top of each bar; when the end-user dragged these knobs up or down, the value of the corresponding element of the array was modified. Graphical editing of pictures was possible because PROVIDE supported only direct views of data structures; synthetic views, crucial to algorithm animation, were not part of the system's design.

Two other aspects of PROVIDE are worth describing. First, the user was able to advance (reverse) in the execution database using arbitrary Boolean expressions to describe and select interesting states of the computation. For example, `active(fie)&&(x==y)` would move the execution to the next (previous) invocation of function `fie` during which variables `x` and `y` were equal. Second, whenever the user changed the value of a variable or code, the system figured out how far back to unroll the database of execution until the changes in the entities no longer affected the results. With the mainframe's computing support, the end-user had the illusion of an interpretive environment.

Only very simple diagrams of simple, non-dynamic, non-user-defined variables were reported, primarily because pictures were extremely difficult to program. PROVIDE, like Incense, PV, and GDBX, was not well-suited for algorithm animation, because it could only monitor data.

2.3 Algorithm Animation Systems

In this section, we look at systems developed explicitly to illustrate algorithms. The first such systems were built at the University of Toronto in the mid–'70s by Baecker and his students. Because of hardware limitations, the systems were not interactive, but were geared to making movies. Their theme was to keep the structure of the original algorithm intact. Our BALSA–I system at Brown, begun in the early '80s, was aimed at the real-time display of a wide variety of algorithms; it also dealt with issues of the user interface and style of interaction. Shortly thereafter, London and Duisberg at Tektronix animated a number of algorithms following the BALSA paradigm; they did not build a hand-crafted system, but used many of Smalltalk's built-in paradigms. We conclude this section by looking at two recent systems also influenced by BALSA–I: Duisberg's Animus and Bentley and Kernighan's Movie/Stills at Bell Labs.

Toronto

In the mid–'70s, much work was done at the University of Toronto under Baecker's direction in the area of algorithm animation [7]. Initially special-purpose animations were made of particular classes of algorithms, using a common library of subroutines to access a keyframe animation package designed for making films. The work included "M. Alcorn ... graphically representing a bubble sort ... S. Sullivan ... a complex tournaments replacement tape sort ... J. Wheeler ... the switchyard algorithm for converting infix expressions into Polish postfix form ... C. D. Romano ... the Warnock non-deterministic hidden line elimination algorithm" [6].

A number of systems were then developed to animate arbitrary programs. The two most relevant here are Yarwood's system "for illustrating programs" [74], and de Boer's system "for animating micro-PL/I programs" [22]. Both of these systems took as input a PL/I program in which some additional information was specified either through pseudo-comments (e.g., "/*/ ... /*/") or through JCL. This allowed the algorithms to be compiled both by the normal PL/I compiler and also by their own systems. Using the pseudo-comments or JCL, their systems generated a version of the original program augmented with additional calls to an animation package. This augmented program was then compiled using the standard PL/I compiler and linked with an animation package.

Yarwood

In Yarwood's system, the programmer prepared a separate JCL file containing *display specifications*: the name of a procedure or a labeled section of code, and a list of variables. The final result of running the augmented program was hardcopy output showing the program text with pictures of the variables. Only scalars, one-dimensional arrays, and indices into one-dimensional arrays could be displayed. The complete set of interesting variables would be displayed each time any of them changed within the specified procedure or labeled section of code. In order to prevent the user from being inundated with displays (for example, running Quicksort on an array of 15 elements typically resulted in over a hundred displays!), a Boolean condition could be specified which controlled when the hardcopy displays were generated.

A fragment of the specification file for Quicksort is as follows:

```
...
*SPEC
  FLOWGROUP = NLEQK;
  CONDITIONAL = (L=1 AND U=13);
  ARRAY A(20) POINTERS (L,U,N,K)
    VALUE
    LABEL A(J) BY
      (N<=J AND J<=K : '?',
        A(J)<=A(L):'<=A(L)', A(J)>A(L):'>A(L)');
...
```

This specification causes the section of code labeled *NLEQK* to be displayed only when variable *L* has a value of 1 and variable *U* has a value of 13. The hardcopy output consists of the array *A* with the four index variables *L*, *U*, *N*, and *K*. Each index variable is displayed in a separate box in a row above the array with a line showing the element of the array it is indexing. The array *A* is displayed as a rectangular box with 20 cells and two rows. The bottom row contains the value of each array element, and the top row contains a textual label for each cell indicating when the corresponding array element is larger or smaller than a particular element. Adjacent cells with identical labels are coalesced in order to show which parts of the array have common characteristics.

For its time, Yarwood's system was a departure from the strictly textual traces of variables prevalent at that time. Its limitations were that only a few types of basic data structures could be monitored, the graphics used in the displays was primitive, and specifying which variables to monitor and how to label them was complex.

De Boer

In de Boer's system, the programmer had greater flexibility in the animations that could be produced. Associated with the declaration of each PL/I variable of interest was some code that specified how the variable should be displayed each time it was updated while the program ran. Consider the following fragment of code from an animation of Selection sort:

```
...
DECLARE (M) FIXED;
  /*/ PICTURE(CIRCLE,
      175+M*150, 450, 100, 100, 24, FADE, 36, 12) /*/
DECLARE (J) FIXED;
  /*/ PICTURE(
      IF J=0 OR J=M OR J=N+1 THEN (BLANK) ELSE (CIRCLE),
      175+J*150, 450, 125, 125, 24, FADE, 36, 12) /*/
DECLARE (A(1:4)) FIXED;
  /*/ PICTURE(CHARS, 175+INDEX*150,
      IF J=N+1 AND INDEX=I THEN (300) ELSE (450),
      55, 75, 24,
      IF PHASE=1 THEN (CUT) ELSE (INTERP),
      IF PHASE=2 THEN (6) ELSE (36), 12) /*/
...
```

Variable A is the array being sorted, I the current pass, M the index of the smallest element on the current pass, and J the element to be compared when looking for the minimum. Variable M is displayed as a circle of radius 100 drawn at position $(175 + M * 150, 450)$, whereas variable J is either a circle of radius 125 at position $(175 + J * 150, 450)$, or invisible. Both graphical objects will be displayed with an intensity of 24 and will fade in from their old picture over 36 movie frames, and the new image will last for 12 frames. The elements of the array are displayed as text, at the horizontal row starting at either $Y = 300$ or $Y = 450$. The variable $PHASE$ is introduced in the algorithm for the purpose of animation. It indicates whether the algorithm is displaying the variables for the first time (in which case they should appear immediately) or during processing (in which case the new value should be interpolated from the old value). One could specify dependencies of variables, so that when a particular variable was modified, the pictures of all of its dependent variables were also redisplayed.

This system provided a way for programmers to augment monitors with additional information about the activity in the algorithm. This takes the forms of the **WAIT**, **ALTER**, and **CONTINUE** commands, and are illustrated in the following section of Selection sort code:

```
    ...
    /*/ WAIT /*/
    /*/ ALTER(M, BLANK, 100,100,10,10,10,FADE,36,12) /*/
    IF M != I
      THEN DO; T=A(I); A(I)=A(M); A(M)=T; END;
      ELSE DO; /*/ ALTER(A(I),CHARS,
        175+I*150,300,55,75,24,INTERP,36,12) /*/ END;
    /*/ CONTINUE /*/
    ...
```

The WAIT command causes the graphics package to batch up all instructions until the next CONTINUE command. The ALTER command causes the variable specified to be redisplayed (until the next time it changes) using the given specification rather than the specifications associated with the declaration of the variable.

The code above exchanges the Mth and the Ith elements; the Ith element is displayed differently because after the exchange, its contents are finalized. At that time, the following events happen simultaneously over the next 36 frames: the circle usually used to show the value of M fades away; the values of the Ith and Mth elements of the arrays dissolve from their old values to their new ones; and the Ith element moves down from $Y = 450$ to $Y = 300$. The ALTER command for $A(I)$ is used when no exchange is needed but the Ith element is to be redisplayed at the lowered position.

De Boer's system attains a compromise between associating monitors with variables (total automation) and inserting graphics calls (no automation). He realized that to obtain good pictures of the program activity, additional semantics must be added to the algorithm. He does this in two ways: ghost variables, that is, variables that are not needed by a non-animated version of the code; and the WAIT and CONTINUE commands to group multiple changes of variables to be displayed as an atomic algorithm event. The ALTER command is essentially a shorthand for ghost variables. The drawbacks of de Boer's approach are that the picture specifications are complex (required for movie-making) and, more seriously, are intertwined with the algorithm. Specifying graphics within a program does not extend to multiple views. De Boer's system did not consider variables other than scalars and one-dimensional arrays. Finally, since the system was intended to produce movies, it did not address any user interface issues.

BALSA–I

Our work in this thesis, begun with the BALSA–I system in the early '80s, is perhaps best described as bringing the movie *Sorting Out Sorting* to life: rather than sorting algorithms, we wanted to animate any and all algorithms; rather than three-year turnaround, we wanted three-minute or even three-second turnaround; rather than a passive movie, we wanted a dynamic interactive environment.

We will not describe BALSA–I here, but will instead analyze what features of which systems were incorporated: i.e., what ideas from each system were borrowed, modified, or intentionally ignored. An interactive algorithm animation environment has three primary aspects: how a programmer builds an animation, how an end-user interacts with it, and how special types of end-users, script readers and script writers, create, modify, and view dynamic documents. Issues relating to scripts are discussed in Chapter 4. The other two are discussed here.

Unquestionably, BALSA–I's interactive environment is most directly influenced by Smalltalk [31]. BALSA–I is, as Tesler calls Smalltalk, reactive: "the user tells it what to do and it reacts" [66]. Smalltalk techniques that were imported included overlapping windows, popup menus, and changing the cursor's shape to give detailed feedback. BALSA–II, in contrast, has adopted much of the Macintosh user interface, primarily because it is implemented based on the Macintosh Toolkit. The feature of zooming into a view on a raster display in order to see more detail, as opposed to just making the picture larger, and of simultaneously presenting both detailed and overall views of an object, is patterned after SDMS [34].

BALSA–I programmers annotated algorithms with "interesting events" calls; this concept has been further refined in BALSA–II into algorithm output events and algorithm input events. The events produce an abstraction of the program execution; it was a major departure from the work done at Toronto. Independently, Model's thesis also used a similar notion of "events" for monitoring system behavior [49]. Model proposed using events for: concurrent monitoring, post-execution simulations of the system activity, interrogation of the history, and helping the system to reason about itself. The last goal is most applicable to the AI systems Model was interested in monitoring. The displays of events in Model's system, although implemented on graphical workstations, were not very graphical.

Balzer's EXDAMS [5] provided the idea of giving viewers the *illusion* of running multiple programs—but without multiple processes or changes to the standard compiler—and also of running them backwards, a feature that appeared in *Sorting Out Sorting*. BALSA–I ran each algorithm independently and, like EXDAMS, saved a history of the execution. BALSA–I's execution trace consisted of the names of the interesting events with the parameters it generated when it was run. After the trace was constructed, simultaneous execution was achieved by just advancing through the various execution traces in a round-robin fashion. The illusion of reverse execution was achieved by traversing the execution traces in reverse order and notifying the views of each event with a flag indicating that the graphical effects of the event should be undone. In BALSA–II, multiple programs are run as coroutines, so there is no waiting while execution traces are generated. Also, because of the computational complexity and storage requirements necessary to implement reverse execution, that feature is not currently supported in BALSA–II.

BALSA's structure of algorithms, input generators, and views is clearly patterned after the UNIX notion of pipes and streams. Components do not communicate or even know about what other components exist; they just output information. The BALSA system is responsible for directing information to the appropriate components. In this way, algorithms, input generators, and views can be modularly replaced. Each component also acts as an object in a classical object-oriented programming framework. It responds to a certain messages, i.e., the interesting events. Objects in, say, Smalltalk have only incoming protocols; in BALSA, certain components have outgoing protocols (e.g., algorithms), and other components have both outgoing and incoming protocols (e.g., input generators). We call these interfaces *repertoires* to avoid confusing them with the one-way interfaces in object-oriented programming languages. These notions are just mentioned briefly here; we discuss them in detail in Chapter 5 in the context of BALSA–II's internal structure.

BALSA did not adopt Smalltalk's model-view-controller (MVC) paradigm (see [30] and Chapter 19, "The Trilogy: Classes for Interactive Applications" in [1]), although the two paradigms do have many similarities. Briefly, MVC is the basis for constructing Smalltalk user interfaces; a *model* contains structured information, a *view* shows a picture of the model in a window, and a *controller* coordinates the end-user's actions. Goldberg states [30]:

> [The MVC] provide the message interface for handling the complexi-
> ties of structured graphical layout. They link keyboard actions, cur-
> sor control, and pressing function keys to messages that are sent to
> the View or the model being viewed. The "model" is, of course, any
> object in the system. The particular way we have implemented these
> kinds of objects, supports linking more than one view to the same
> model so that several views of a model can be seen simultaneously.

Clearly, MVC and BALSA both advocate separating the code that computes
the model from the code that displays the model. In the MVC paradigm,
end-users can interact with the model by sending messages to the views.
In BALSA, end-users can interact with an algorithm through a view, but
only when the algorithm requests data. View parameters, introduced in
BALSA–II, affect the way the model is displayed, not the model itself. The
MVC paradigm can be used to simulate BALSA's framework for algorithm
animation, as was done by London and Duisberg at Tektronix; their system
is discussed next.

There is yet another major difference between the philosophies of views
of Smalltalk objects and those of algorithms in BALSA. In Smalltalk, the
view is the object. In BALSA, the algorithm generates an abstract model,
usually without any geometry, as a stream of events. Views are displays
of this abstract model. Moreover, in BALSA–II, views themselves often
generate abstract models (usually revealing properties of themselves) which
are displayed by yet other views.

Another paradigm with similarities to the BALSA framework is what Stefik, Bobrow, and Kahn have recently called *access-oriented programming*
in LOOPS [62]: "In access-oriented programming, fetching or storing data
can cause procedures to be invoked ... when one object changes its data,
a message may be sent as a side effect ... programs are factored into parts
that compute and parts that monitor the computations." Thus, displays in
LOOPS are, by necessity, direct views of program variables. The variables
being monitored are called *active values* and appropriately, displays of them
are called *gauges*. In contrast, to a first approximation, one can think of
BALSA as monitoring not variables but the fundamental operations in an
algorithm, resulting from possibly many accesses and transformations. In
LOOPS, a monitor is associated in one place with a variable; from there on,
all accesses and modifications to that variable cause the monitoring routine
to be invoked. In BALSA, one inserts the interesting event marker at the

point in the algorithm at which the event happens. The notion of views of
views in BALSA–II is similar to LOOPS's notion of *recursive annotations.*

Although we have emphasized the differences between Smalltalk's MVC
and LOOPS's active values, either could, of course, be used as a basis for
algorithm animation or for an algorithm animation system. What they provide "for free," and what an algorithm animation system must consequently
reimplement, is maintaining a dependency of views that are called sequentially to be updated. This is but a small aspect of an algorithm animation
environment. Other aspects, such as a script facility, identifying operations
of interest within an algorithm, and an interpreter integrated with algorithm
operations that runs multiple algorithms, are independent of whether the algorithm animation system or the base language maintains the dependencies.
For animating algorithms, a procedural algorithmic language seems to be a
more logical base language; for presenting complex interactive simulations,
with direct displays of the variables of interest in the simulation, Smalltalk
and LOOPS seems to be very appropriate base languages. As we shall discuss in Chapter 5, a procedural language incorporating some object-oriented
flavors would be ideal for an algorithm animation system.

Finally, the algorithm animation systems at Toronto were very influen-
tial in our early design thinking. They convinced us that monitors of data
structures are insufficient for providing good animations, and that some
modification of code might be needed to yield appropriate displays. They
also convinced us that we needed a mechanism to *describe* what is happen-
ing in the algorithm to an external display, rather than integrating display
algorithms into algorithm being animated. Further, displays are non-trivial
to code; they cannot be described by a few lines of code that are executed
on each variable access or modification. Rather, the global program state
influences how information should be displayed.

Tektronix

London and Duisberg at Tektronix animated a collection of algorithms in
Smalltalk [47] following BALSA's approach of annotating the algorithm with
"interesting events." By using Smalltalk's MVC paradigm, they let the
Smalltalk system notify all views of an object of each event, rather than
maintaining the dependencies themselves.

They noted the following deficiencies with the MVC paradigm when used
for animating algorithms. First, all views are notified sequentially of the

events. If views are incremental, the end-user notices the fact that multiple views are not updated simultaneously. Second, when combining multiple views onto a composite, "the subview hierarchy causes the display to redraw itself repeatedly upon activation of a window." Third, the direct application of MVC does not allow back-mapping of the view to the model. Thus, one could not pick a node in a binary tree and expect the model to realize that a node was picked, or which node was selected. That is because the model does not know how many or what kind of views the end-user has opened; by design, the model just broadcasts a message and the Smalltalk system determines the appropriate dependents.

We discuss the relative advantages and drawbacks of using a general-purpose environment for algorithm animation at the end of this chapter.

Animus

Duisberg, in his recent thesis [23], investigated using *temporal constraints* to "describe the appearance and structure of a picture as well as how those pictures evolve over time." One application of this technique is to algorithm animation. Using temporal constraints allows multiple incremental updates to be done simultaneously rather than sequentially. Constraints are specified externally to the program being animated, by setting up a Smalltalk message as the constraint trigger.

Duisberg stated in a preliminary report of the work [24] that one can "animate unaltered algorithmic code by stating trigger constraints externally." A caveat must be added. The example that Duisberg uses is sorting algorithms, where the implementer of the algorithm has chosen to use messages "compareWith" and "exchangeWith" for performing the algorithm. It is true that by monitoring those messages, the animation is achieved without altering the algorithm. What is not stated is that this is possible only because the triggers to drive the animation happen to coincide with the messages in the algorithm, and that the messages in the program happen to be the appropriate abstractions. Had the algorithm been coded with messages "setValue" rather than "exchangeWith," or with in-line statements rather than messages, unaltered animation would not have been possible.

In general, as discussed in Chapter 1, the triggers to drive an animation do not necessarily coincide with the abstractions in the algorithm (embodied as messages in Smalltalk, or as procedures in Algol-based languages), nor is using abstractions as a triggering mechanism limited to Smalltalk.

Movie/Stills

Bentley and Kernighan [11] at Bell Labs have recently implemented a suite of tools for producing animations of algorithms. They state: "the output is crude, but the system is easy to use; novice users can animate a program in a couple of hours. The system currently produces movies on a Teletype 5620 terminals and Sun workstations and also renders movies into 'stills' that can be included in `troff` documents."

Bentley and Kernighan follow the BALSA paradigm of annotating an algorithm at places that should cause an image to change. There are six types of annotations, called *script primitives*: click, view, and graphics commands to draw lines, circles, boxes, and text. The click primitive designates the name of an *interesting event*; end-users can control the animation and the sequence of stills by specifying conditions based on the clicks. The view primitive specifies that subsequent graphics commands are associated together to be displayed in the same window. Lines can be drawn with arrowheads; circles and boxes can be filled and hollow. The text primitive can also be used to display some simple geometric objects, e.g., bullets. Optionally, the graphics primitives can be labeled to cause the graphics associated with the previous occurrence of that label to be erased. This produces an animation with discrete transformation characteristics (see Chapter 1).

To produce a movie, the algorithm is run, an intermediate file containing the primitives is produced; this file is called a *script*, not be confused with the way we use the term to refer to dynamic documents. The script file is sent, transparently to end-users, to the *develop* filter, which produces an *intermediate* file with a simpler set of graphic primitives. The intermediate file is drawn on the screen by *movie*, or inserted into a `troff` document by the *stills* preprocessor. Movie allows the end-user to specify the size and location where each view should be displayed, the speed of the animation, and whether it should be run forwards or backwards. As in BALSA–I, the illusion of reverse execution is accomplished by displaying the sequence of graphical primitives in reverse order. Movie erases objects by redrawing them in xor-mode or by drawing new objects in and-mode to overwrite the old image. Multiple algorithms can be run together by merging various various script files together using standard UNIX programs before sending the intermediate file to Movie.

This system provides tremendous return for very little effort—on the part of the systems guru. The work that the algorithmatician must do is a bit more difficult than in BALSA: both require the algorithm to be annotated. However, in this system, an additional annotation must be inserted for each and every possible view. Adding a new type of view would require all algorithms to be modified. Moreover, the annotation has quite a bit of graphics-related information in it. One could remedy this deficiency (as the authors point out and give an example) by adopting the convention that rather than outputting script primitives, programs could output the name of the interesting event, or any arbitrary string. A filter can then be built to generate a script by translating each event into appropriate script primitives. Such a filter would function like an adapter in BALSA–II.

Movie/Stills adopts the UNIX theme that "the most fruitful way of enhancing the environment is . . . by using small filters that interact with the various files in the system." Movie/Stills strives to be a simple tool, not a full-blown algorithm animation system; it succeeds in its goals.

2.4 Discussion

Algorithm animation systems have the common characteristic that the interesting phenomena in the algorithm are identified manually. Early systems at Toronto, and naive users of Movie/Stills, insert the graphics directly, whereas BALSA and the systems it influenced use a level of indirection. When the display is limited to a single view, as was the case with the movies generated at Toronto, the level of indirection is extra and unnecessary baggage. However, when multiple views are displayed—either simultaneously or separately—the level of indirection is indispensable. It isolates the algorithm from the details concerning each view, and makes it easy for views to be shared.

Systems that display data structures graphically or that monitor variables graphically or textually do not need algorithms annotated. However, the types of displays that are possible are different from those that can be produced by an algorithm animation system. Which style is more helpful depends on the intended use. Graphical displays of data structures seem better suited to debugging at the statement level, whereas algorithm animation displays are suited to synthesizing and analyzing at a higher level.

An algorithm animation environment is fine-tuned for the particular purpose of investigating the behavior of programs. The goals of an algorithm animation and those of a general-purpose programming environment overlap, but one neither consumes nor subsumes the other.

Using a general-purpose environment in lieu of an algorithm animation system, as London and Duisberg did, especially one as rich and interactive as Smalltalk, has the advantage that the algorithm animation system can be built trivially. To the programmer implementing the animation, there is little difference in the way he annotates algorithms and implements views. However, to the end-user there is a major difference.

The primary drawback of using a general-purpose programming environment is that end-users are restricted to using only those features found in the environment. In particular, end-users cannot run multiple algorithms in parallel, they cannot control the speed (except by single-stepping), they cannot code algorithms in an algorithmic languages (although some might claim that describing algorithms Smalltalk is a better approach), they cannot see views in independent windows or zoom into a view, they cannot run algorithms backwards, they have no notion of scripts, and so on. Clearly, these features could be built into a general-purpose environment; as suggested in Chapter 1, doing so would greatly enhance them.

3

The Interactive Environment

A substantial portion of the research reported here concerns the nature of the interactive environment for exploring animated algorithms. In this chapter, we present a "tour" through BALSA–II from an end-user's perspective. The first half of the tour shows the common facilities for all end-users, and the second half shows specialized facilities that are typically used only by advanced end-users studying algorithms in detail. After this, we present a model underlying the interactive environment.

BALSA–II currently runs on a Macintosh, and has tailored the Macintosh user interface [2] for algorithm animation using our experience with the BALSA–I system. This chapter assumes some familiarity with the basic Mac user interface, including *pull-down menus*, *grow icons*, and *dialog boxes*, as well as general workstation terminology, such as *double-clicking*, *windows*, and *dragging*.

The diagrams that follow cannot, of course, give the "feel" of the interactive environment, but they indicate most of what can be done with it. Keep it in mind that BALSA–II is domain-independent. We use common algorithms and fairly obvious displays to enable to the reader to concentrate on the environment and systems aspects, not on understanding the algorithms.

3.1 Basic Tour

Upon entering BALSA–II, we picked **Selection Sort** from the **Algs** menu and start running it using the **Go** command in the **Run** menu. We can suspend the algorithm at any time by a mouse click, and resume it using **Go** again.

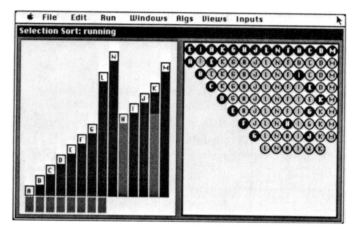

Figure 3.1

The **Sticks** view on the left in Figure 3.1 represents the array being sorted as a set of sticks whose heights correspond to their values, with a rectangle drawn beneath a stick when it is processed. The stick highlighted in gray is the current minimum. A gray mask, whose height corresponds to the value of the current minimum, slides to the right as each of the remaining elements of the array is considered.

The **Compare-Exchange** view on the right represents comparisons by gray circles and exchanges by black ones. A row is started each time an array element is processed, thereby showing a history of the comparisons and exchanges.

The fact that Selection sort is an N^2 algorithm can be easily verified by the number of elements in the **Compare-Exchange** view: ignoring the top row that shows the initial contents of the array, there will ultimately be $N - 1$ rows with the ith row containing $N - i$ compare operations and 1 exchange operation. Thus, we have

$$\sum_{1 \le i \le N-1} N - i + 1 = \frac{N(N+1)}{2} - 1 = O(N^2).$$

Alternatively, one can make the following geometric argument: there are $N(N-1)$ potential icons (again, we ignore the top row), and a bit more that half of those will be filled with icons representing program operations.

Figure 3.2

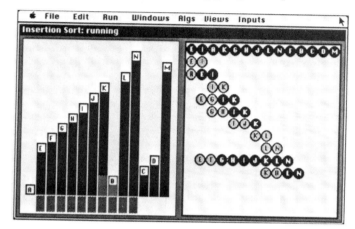

Figure 3.2 shows the screen after we have chosen **Insertion Sort** from the **Algs** menu. The differences between Insertion sort and Selection sort are fairly evident in the **Compare-Exchange** view.

Figure 3.3

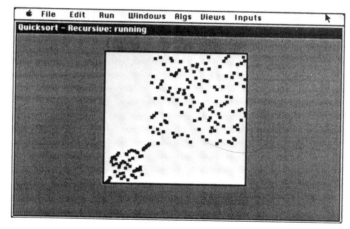

The default display for Quicksort, shown in Figure 3.3, operates on a much larger set of data than Insertion or Selection sorts. The **Dots** view displays a dot for each element of the array being sorted: the horizontal coordinate corresponds to its position in the array, and the vertical corresponds to its value. One can think of the dots as the tops of the sticks in the **Sticks** view from above.

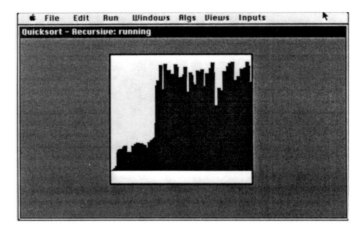

Figure 3.4

In fact, by selecting **Sticks** from the **Views** menus, we have the familiar **Sticks** view shown in Figure 3.4. Because there is a lot of data, the sticks overlap, and the distinctive rectangular blocks dots, corresponding to subfiles waiting to be processed, are no longer visible.

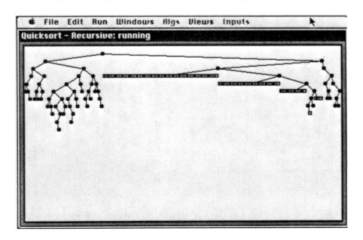

Figure 3.5

Other views can illustrate different aspects of the algorithm. The Partition-Tree view in Figure 3.5 displays each array element as a node in the tree whose horizontal coordinate corresponds to its position in the array.

Circular nodes have been used as partitioning elements, and their depths in the tree reflect when each was used as the partitioning element. The contiguous square nodes represent subfiles that are waiting to be processed; their depths indicate when each was put on the stack awaiting processing.

Watching the dynamics of the tree being built reveals that Quicksort is processing the smaller subfile before the larger one.

Figure 3.6

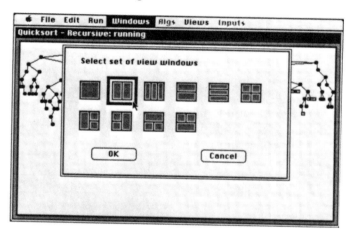

In order to see more than one view of Quicksort simultaneously, we use the View Windows command in the Windows menu. The dialog box in Figure 3.6 contains icons for the available ways to tile the screen with view windows. We can choose one of the arrangements by selecting it followed by OK, or by just double-clicking.

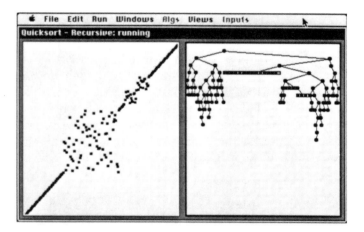

Figure 3.7

Figure 3.7 shows the screen after we have chosen the new configuration of view windows, specified which view should go into the new window, and let the program run some more. As the program runs, all views are updated simultaneously and are therefore consistent representations of the algorithm and its data structures.

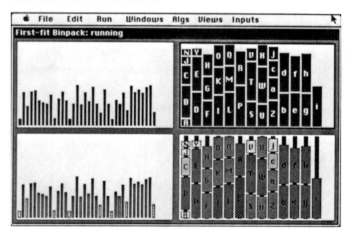

Figure 3.8

In Figure 3.8, we have switched from sorting to binpacking algorithms. (The binpacking problem is to arrange a set of weights into the fewest number of bins possible, subject to the constraint that each bin has a capacity that may not be exceeded.)

In Figure 3.8, there are two instantiations each of the **Weights** view and of the **Packing** view. The **Weights** view displays each weight as a stick whose height corresponds to its value. The weights in this algorithm are distributed between 0 and .5, where each bin has a capacity of 1. The **Packing** view shows how the weights are arranged in each bin; within each bin, each new weight is drawn above the weights already in the bin.

Attributes of each view can be controlled through the **Parms** command in the **View** menu. The view parameters for these displays are whether or not to display each weight in solid black, or to assign a color to the weight corresponding to its magnitude relative to the bin's capacity. The **Packing** view also has a view parameter that causes a solid black stick to be drawn representing the capacity of each non-empty bin.

There are two types of windows: algorithm and view windows. All figures, including this one, have shown exactly one algorithm window that happens to comprise the entire screen except the menu bar. Double-clicking on a window causes its "window dressing" to be drawn or erased, if it is currently displayed. View window dressing consists of a title bar, three scroll bars, and various icons; algorithm window dressing consists of a number in the upper right corner indicating how much "time" the algorithm has consumed.

Figure 3.9

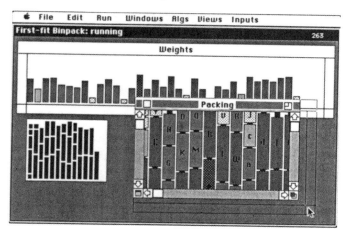

Figure 3.9 shows the screen from before after we have rearranged some views windows and are in the midst of changing the size of one of them. Clicking in a view window "selects" that window: it is brought to the top of the pile of (potentially) overlapping windows and its border is highlighted.

Following Macintosh conventions, the title bar is used for moving windows, the close box (left edge of title bar) for removing windows from the screen, and the expand box (right edge of title bar) for expanding a window to its maximum size, moving it to the top left of the algorithm window (overlapping any other view windows in the process), and rescaling the contents to fit the new size. If the window is already "expanded," clicking the expand box returns the window to its previous location and rescales the contents. Changing the size of a window, except through the expand box, does not cause the contents to be rescaled; it just controls how much of the underlying view can be seen.

The rescale box in the lower left corner rescales the view to fit the current view window. In standard computer graphics terminology, rescaling causes the entire "window" onto the "world coordinate system" to be displayed such that it fills the entire view window. The view window can be thought of as a differentially scaled version of the "normalized device coordinates."

When the window is small or the amount of data is large it is displayed in miniature. We can enlarge parts of the display by using the zoom scroll bar on the left of the view window, and can scroll through the display using the scroll bars at the right and the bottom.

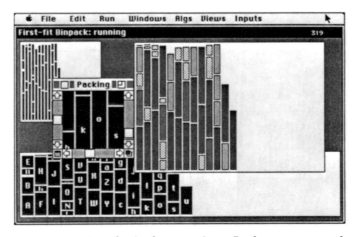

Figure 3.10

Zooming is a logical operation. It does not merely magnify the pixels on the screen, but rather causes more and more information to be displayed. The nature of the additional information depends on the view. Figure 3.10

shows the screen with four instantiations of the Packing view; all but the topmost view have been rescaled to fit their current windows.

Figure 3.11

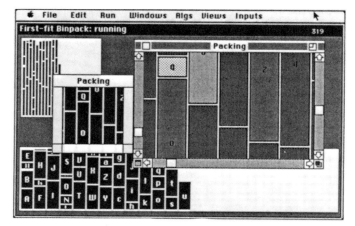

Figure 3.11 shows the same set of windows as before, but with different zooming and scrolling. Bringing the zoom bar's thumb to the very bottom of the zoom scroll bar quadruples the size of the image while keeping the center point of the picture stationary. This also forces the thumb to be repositioned at the center of the zoom bar, so that the image can be enlarged or reduced again. We can get a feel for what part of the entire view is currently being displayed by the position of the thumbs in the zoom and panning scroll bars.

Figure 3.12

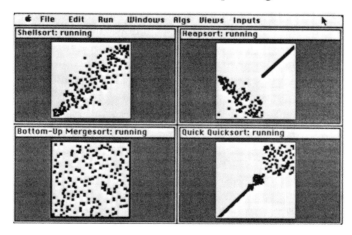

Just as we can tile an algorithm window with view windows, so can we tile the screen with algorithm windows. Figure 3.12 shows the screen with four sorting algorithms running simultaneously. Algorithm windows cannot be moved, sized, or deleted; rather, a new tiling strategy for the screen is chosen. The static picture of the dots is very distinctive, but the dynamics are even more so.

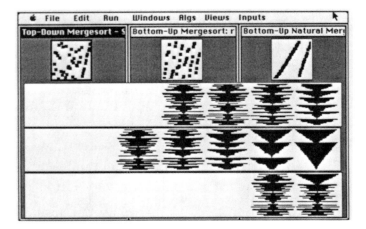

Figure 3.13

A view window is not constrained to be completely contained inside of its algorithm window; however, it cannot be moved completely outside of its "parent" algorithm window. Thus, contrived configurations such as Figure 3.13 are possible, though they rarely occur in practice.

There is always a "selected" view window (the topmost) which belongs to the "selected" algorithm window; clicking in an algorithm window causes it and its most recently selected view to become the ones selected.

Algorithm windows always appear below *all* view windows. View windows in each algorithm window are contiguous in their top-to-bottom ordering. Using the scripting facility described in Chapter 4, we can create a complex configuration of windows and save (restore) them into (from) a file.

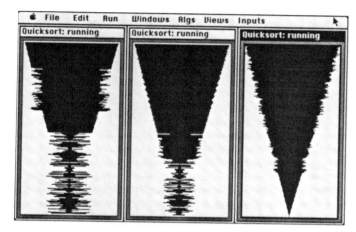

Figure 3.14

There are two types of inputs to a program: data that the algorithm manipulates (e.g., an array of numbers) and parameters that tune the algorithm (e.g., an increment sequence to use for Shellsort). Figure 3.14 shows the effect of different algorithm parameters on the same algorithm operating on the same set of data. The version of Quicksort at the far left is the naive version ($M = 1$); the middle version uses Insertion sort for small subfiles ($M = 7$), and the rightmost version uses a larger cutoff for subfiles ($M = 25$).

The HBars view in Figure 3.14 displays each element of the array as a horizontal bar whose length corresponds to the element's value. When the array is sorted, a filled in V will result.

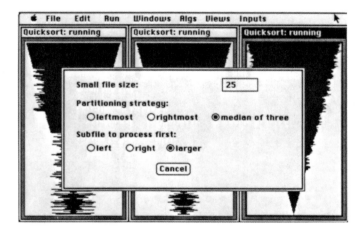

Figure 3.15

The dialog box in Figure 3.15 shows the parameters available for tuning Quicksort programs. These include the criterion for choosing the size of "small" subfiles which are sorted using Insertion sort, the strategy for picking a partitioning element, and which subfile to process first.

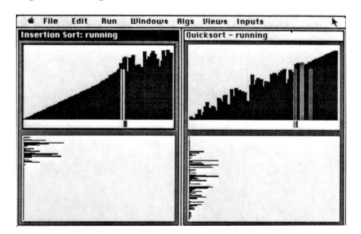

Figure 3.16

Up to now, we have been sorting an array containing a random permutation. Other input generators for sorting algorithms include a random set of integers (this allows duplicate keys), an increasing or decreasing set of numbers, and a set of numbers stored in a file. In Figure 3.16, we are running

Quicksort and Insertion sort on the same file, one that is initially "almost sorted;" Insertion sort isn't doing too badly!

The Inversion Table view at the bottom of each algorithm window indicates how close each element of the array is to being sorted. More precisely, the stick for element i has length proportional to j if there are j elements larger than the ith element in positions 1 through $i - 1$.

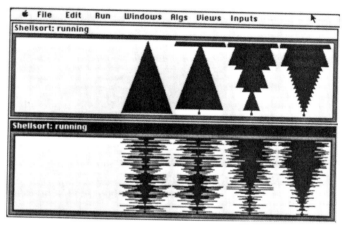

Figure 3.17

It is also useful to run the identical algorithm simultaneously on different input models. In Figure 3.17, Shellsort on top is running on a set of numbers in decreasing order; on the bottom, it is running on a random set of numbers.

In the HBars-History view, the column of bars at the far right corresponds to the current contents of the array being sorted. A copy of the view is made and slid to the left when each Shellsort increment in processed.

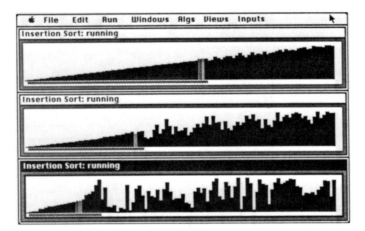

Figure 3.18

Input parameters govern the type of data that an input generator provides to the algorithm. For example, in Figure 3.18, the same algorithm, Insertion sort, is running with the same input model generator, **Almost Sorted**, but each instantiation has different values for the input generator parameters. It is clear from the static display that Insertion sort performs well when the file is close to being sorted.

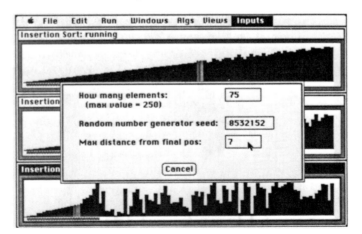

Figure 3.19

The parameters for input generator **Almost Sorted** are: the size of the array to sort, a seed for the random number generator to use, and how "almost sorted" the array should be (i.e., each element is no more than K units from its final destination). The dialog box that allows us to set these values is shown in Figure 3.19.

The values of the algorithm and input generator parameters cannot be changed while programs are running; only before they start. However, the values of the parameters can be observed while the programs are running; thus, Figures 3.15 and 3.19 each contain a **Cancel** button (but not an **OK**).

Figure 3.20

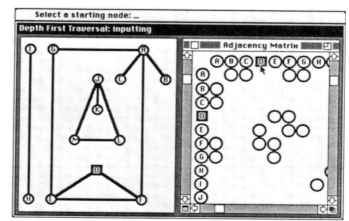

Some data for some algorithms cannot be specified until the algorithm begins running. For example, an animation involving insertions and deletions in a balanced tree might prompt the end-user to specify a node to be deleted. Or, as shown in Figure 3.20, a graph traversal algorithm prompts the end-user to select a vertex at which the traversal will begin.

Information specified by the end-user while the algorithm is running is called a runtime-specific. This information can be specified textually (e.g., the end-user could type a letter in response to the prompt in the menu bar), or graphically (e.g., the end-user could use the mouse to click on an object corresponding to a vertex in any of the views). Obviously, graphical input is not necessarily meaningful in every view because not all views contain direct representations of data structures.

It is important to realize that the end-user cannot give such information to the algorithm at all times. It is specified only in response to a request by the algorithm. Algorithm and input generator parameters, on the other hand, can be specified at any time before the algorithm starts running, and view parameters can be specified any time at all.

3.2 Advanced Tour

The remainder of the tour illustrates features of BALSA–II geared to the algorithm specialist. Some familiarity with our model of animating algorithms is assumed. Readers might find it helpful to skim the "Conceptual Model" section in Chapter 1 before proceeding.

As described in Chapter 1, fundamental to BALSA–II is the notion of an "algorithm event." Output events correspond to an operation performed by the algorithm, and input events correspond to an algorithm's request for data. For example, graph algorithms use the output events "visit node" and "remember node" (corresponding to when a vertex has been visited and when it is put on the stack or queue to be visited later), and input events "get edge" and "get node."

Events are essential both to programmers implementing algorithms, input generators, and views and to the end-users watching the algorithms in action.

For the programmer, output events are the vehicle through which algorithms communicate with views. When an output event is encountered in the algorithm, all views are notified of the event and they update themselves appropriately based on the type of the event and the parameters to the event. Analogously, algorithms and input generators communicate using input events.

For the end-user, events are important because it is through them that he controls the execution and synchronization of algorithms.

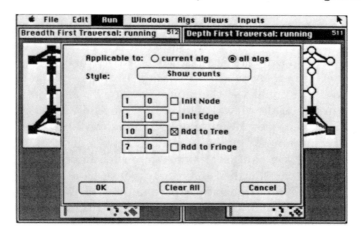

Figure 3.21

The dialog box in Figure 3.21 shows the events for graph traversal algorithms. (For historical reasons, only the algorithm output events are shown.) The check box to the left of each event indicates whether that event is in the set of events that constitute the next "step." The value to its left indicates how many events of that type should occur before a "stop" occurs. At the far left is the "cost" assigned to it.

BALSA–II schedules the multiple algorithms in a round-robin fashion. During each time-slice, an algorithm executes until it reaches an event and then that event is broadcast by BALSA–II to all views so they can update themselves. If the cost for the event is W, then that algorithm misses its next $W - 1$ time-slices.

Two additional terms are helpful: the *event count* of an algorithm is the number of events that have occurred, and the *virtual time* is the weighted sum of the events. More precisely, let $W(e)$ represent the cost associated with event e, let $N(e)$ be the number of times event e occurs when an algorithm is run, and let E be the set of events that the algorithm contains. The event count and the virtual time are computed as follows:

$$C = \sum_{\forall j \in E} N(j), \qquad \text{and} \qquad T = \sum_{\forall j \in E} N(j)W(j).$$

It follows directly from BALSA–II's scheduling algorithm that while multiple algorithms are running, their virtual times are identical. However, their event counts may not be. It is the virtual time, not the event count, that is displayed as part of the algorithm window dressing.

Figure 3.22 illustrates graphically the effects of assigning costs with events. Quicksort was run three times on the same set of 25 items, shown in the figure as circles, squares, and triangles. The particular implementation of Quicksort contains three events corresponding to exchanges (filled symbols), comparisons (gray symbols), and starting the partitioning phase (hollow symbols). The cost associated with the events in each run is indicated by the elongation of the symbol; their numeric values are as follows:

	Partition	Comparison	Exchange
Circles:	10	10	10
Rectangles:	30	7	14
Triangles:	30	7	5

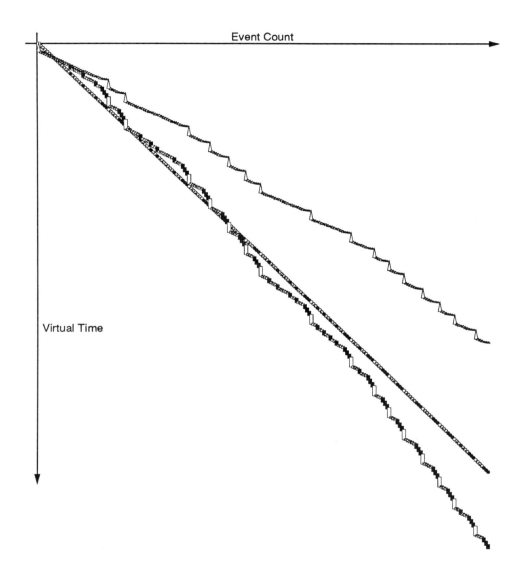

Figure 3.22: *Effects of associating costs with events.*

The event count is displayed along the horizontal axis, and virtual time along the vertical axis. Of the three models, the second (rectangles) probably models current hardware most accurately.

Figure 3.23

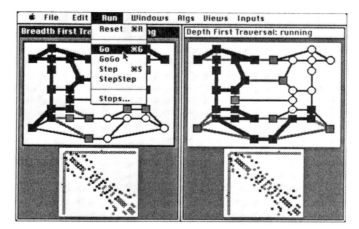

Following MacPascal terminology, algorithms can be run in one of four styles: Go stops at the next stoppoint; GoGo pauses at stoppoints; Step stops at the next steppoint; and StepStep pauses at steppoints. The Reset command terminates the execution of the selected algorithm. See Figure 3.23.

Figure 3.24

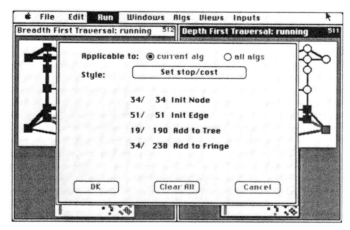

The dialog box in Figure 3.24 is displayed as a result of selecting the appropriate option in the dialog box from before. The dialog box shows the number of times each event has occurred, the sum of which equals the algorithm's event count, as well as its weighted count, the sum of which equals the algorithm's virtual time.

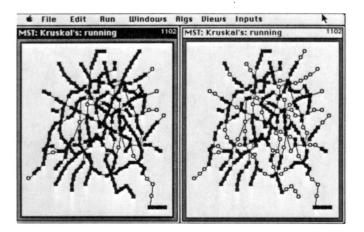

Figure 3.25

Figure 3.25 shows two instantiations of Kruskal's algorithm for finding a minimal spanning tree in an undirected graph. Both versions have the same parameters, input generators and so on, but they have progressed at different rates because different costs have been assigned to the events. This is useful for simulating the algorithm on two different models of computation.

3.3 Model of the Interactive Environment

End-users can use only those algorithms, views, and input generators that client programmers have previously implemented. The collection of such pieces are stored in a database called the *World*. It contains: an executable version of the source code and a unique name by which end-users refer to to each algorithm, view, and input generator; the relationships among them (i.e., which input generators can be used with which algorithms); and information about each algorithm event (i.e., its name and its default step, stop, and cost values).

Recall that an end-user is always in a "setup-run" loop. In the setup phase, he arranges the screen and decides which algorithms to run, which input generator and views to use, and what the values of parameters to each of these should be. In the run phase, he executes the algorithms and watches them through the views on the screen. While algorithms are running, the end-user can suspend them to change the ensemble of views, as well as the events' step, stop, and cost values. These notions are formalized as follows:

▶ *The attributes that comprise the setup are called* structural *properties; those that concern the speed and breakpoints are called* temporal *properties; and those that pertain to how the algorithm is displayed visually are called* presentation *properties.* ◀

We say that the system is *unstable* when any algorithm on the screen is in the middle of running; it is *stable* otherwise.

Structural properties are set while the system is stable—except for the runtime specifics; temporal and presentation properties can be set at any time. In practice, end-users quickly acclimate themselves to the "setup-run" style of interaction and come to regard as natural the distinction between commands used in the setup phase (structural) and those in the run phase (temporal and presentation). For example, if an end-user hits the mouse to pause the running algorithms, it seems reasonable that at this point he can also change what views are on the screen or what breakpoints are in effect; however, it does not make sense to change, say, which data file a file compression algorithm is using, or the size of nodes in a B-tree algorithm. If the end-user really wanted to change the data file or the size of nodes, he would first terminate the current running of the algorithm causing the system to go into a stable mode.

At any given time, an *image* or *snapshot* of the environment is defined by the contents of the *World*, the structural, temporal, and presentation properties, and its *runtime state*. Intuitively, the runtime state represents how far each algorithm has executed.

Structural Properties

The structural properties of the environment are the structural state of the algorithm windows on the screen. This can be expressed formally as follows:

▶ *The* structural properties *of an algorithm animation environment at a particular time are the set* $\{A_1, \ldots, A_M\}$, *where*

> M *is the number of algorithm windows on the screen, and*
> A_i *is the structural state of the ith algorithm.* ◀

The structural state of an algorithm consists of information that can affect the runtime behavior of the algorithm. For example, a file compression algorithm is affected by what file is input but is not affected by, say, the location of view windows on the screen.

The complete set of structural information for an algorithm is as follows:

▶ *The structural state of an algorithm A is the set $\{D_A, P, X, I\}$, where*
  D_A *identifies algorithm A in The World database,*
   P *are A's parameters,*
   X *are external resources A uses, and*
   I *is the structural state of the input generator.* ◀

Data manipulated by an algorithm is usually provided by the input generator. However, algorithms can also use external resources directly. For example, a file compression algorithm might use a database of the frequency of words appearing in Shakespeare's plays.

The input generator has no presentation or temporal states. It has only a structural state containing the following information:

▶ *The structural state of an input generator I is the set $\{D_I, P, X, R\}$, where*
  D_I *identifies input generator I in The World database,*
   P *are I's parameters,*
   X *are external resources I uses, and*
   R *are I's runtime specifics.* ◀

An input generator's external resources are typically the data files the input generator uses for providing data to algorithms. Rarely does an input generator itself need external resources. The runtime specifics are like parameters except they are not specified before the algorithm begins but they are specified while the program starts running in response to code in the algorithm requesting information.

Temporal Properties

The temporal state of the environment is the temporal state of each of the M algorithms. This consists of the following information concerning how each algorithm event should be processed:

▶ *The temporal state of an algorithm is the set $\{E_1, \ldots, E_{|E|}\}$, where E_i is the step, stop, and cost values associated with the ith event.* ◀

The set of events for each algorithm is found in The World database.

Presentation Properties

The presentation state of the environment is the presentation state of each of the M algorithms, along with one specially designated window called the *selected algorithm*, α. Each algorithm is displayed in an algorithm window on the screen, and the selected algorithm is displayed differently from the other algorithm windows. This distinction is an important one because many commands apply only to the currently selected algorithm. The presentation state of each algorithm is as follows:

▶ *The presentation state of an algorithm is the set* $\{W, V_1, \ldots, V_K, \vartheta\}$, *where*
  W *describes the window on the screen,*
  K *is the number of view windows currently in the algorithm window,*
  V_i *is the presentation state of the ith view, and*
  ϑ *is the selected view.* ◀

The algorithm window contains the coordinates of the window, a flag indicating whether or not the window dressing should be displayed, and a way to access the workstation environment's notion of the window. The window coordinates are relative to the size of the "desktop": the part of the screen that the algorithm animation environment can use. Thus, environments that are identical in terms of structural, temporal, and presentation states would be displayed differently on different-sized desktops.

Each of an algorithm's K views is displayed in a view window on the screen, and one of these is designated as the *selected view*, ϑ. The selected view is the topmost window among its algorithm's windows. It is displayed differently when the algorithm is the selected algorithm. Consequently, only one view window is displayed as a selected window on the screen at any given time. Whenever the selected algorithm changes, the selected view also changes. Again, the concept of the selected view is important because many commands affect only that view. Unlike some multi-window applications where only the topmost window is "active," all views in an algorithm animation environment are updated simultaneously as the algorithm to which they are attached executes. Only one window, the selected view window, has the input focus, however. A view window has no structural state; it has only the following presentation state:

▶ *The presentation state of a view V is the set $\{D_V, P, X, W\}$, where*
  D_V *identifies view V in The World database,*
   P *are V's parameters,*
   X *are the external resources V uses, and*
   W *describes the window on the screen.* ◀

Typical resources that a view uses are fonts. The state of a view window is more complex than the state of an algorithm window: in addition to the location (also stored relative to the size of its parent window), dressing flag, and pointer to the workstation environment's notion of the window, it also contains the current zooming factor, the current horizontal and vertical scroll amounts, and the previous location (used for implementing the expand feature).

3.4 Summary

In this thesis we are concerned not with making movies of algorithms in action but with interactive environments for exploring their behavior. Thus, the interactive environment described in this chapter is not a peripheral part of this dissertation. It is paramount.

The importance of the model of the environment will become clearer in later chapters. When we discuss how script authors and script viewers build and interact with scripts in Chapter 4, a rigorous model of the environment is indispensable for identifying the semantics of end-user actions. When we discuss how algorithmaticians implement algorithms and input generators and how animators implement views in Chapters 5, the model of how end-users can interact with each component is vital for understanding how and why the various components are structured as they are. Finally, when we discuss the system implementation in Chapter 6, we see that many of the fundamental data structures map directly to the properties we have defined here. In fact, one can view the algorithm animation system itself as merely a user interface to the set of "abstract" properties defined here. BALSA–II happens to be one such user interface; others are certainly possible.

4

Scripts

Scripts have proven to be useful in many capacities and we believe that they can be equally important in a wide variety of interactive systems.† Although an algorithm animation system has its own peculiarities and the way in which scripts are integrated into BALSA–II is certainly not independent of the system, the tradeoffs we evaluate are applicable, we believe, to the design of interactive systems in general.

In this chapter, we present an overview of what scripts are and how they can be used in a number of areas. We then review related work and describe BALSA–II's user interface for the script author and script viewer. Following that, we describe and evaluate the tradeoffs to be considered when designing a script facility. We conclude this chapter with a section evaluating our design decisions, and indicate some areas for future work.

4.1 Overview

A script is a record of an end-user's session that can be stored on disk and replayed by another end-user. We call the end-user a *script author* when he has instructed the system to record his session, and we call the end-user a *script viewer* when he has instructed the system to replay a script. We call the actual file that records a session a *transcript* file, and we use the term *script* to refer to the hierarchical arrangement of transcript files.

---

† In fact, there are commercial products, such as Tempo from Affinity Microsystems, Ltd. for the Macintosh, that save keystrokes and mouse-clicks into a file that the end-user can replay by a pressing single control key. While our notion of scripts aims at much higher-level macros, the recent appearance of such products supports our belief that scripts have wide applicability.

At the lowest level, a script is composed of *units*, the boundaries of which correspond to the points at which the script author finished modifying the structural, temporal, and presentation aspects of the environment in the "setup" phase, and began the "run" phase. Units are grouped to form a *scene*, and scenes are grouped to form a *chapter*. Thus, chapters and scenes organize the units, but it is the units that contain the material to be viewed. Multiple scripts covering the same material, in a different order or level of detail, are thus easy to develop because they will share many units.

Although a viewer typically watches the script in the sequence that the author designated, on occasion clicking the mouse to indicate he is ready for the next part, a script is not merely a "virtual videotape" of an end-user's actions. The viewer can also browse through the script in any order, jumping as desired to units within the current scene or to a different scene within the current chapter. Moreover, the viewer can customize the display of the information by altering the temporal and presentation properties of the algorithms that are running. Thus, the script can be thought of as a framework for presenting material—one that can be customized by the viewer.

Scripts are created by instructing the system to "watch what I do." However, the transcript file is not a simple recording of the author's keystrokes or commands. It need not be recorded, for instance, that the author created three windows, then moved two of them, deleted one and then decided to recreate it. What is important is where the three windows on the screen were located and what views and algorithms were inside them when the author began running the program. More specifically, it is the structural, temporal, and presentation states of the environment, and the changes to them, that are saved.

A novel aspect of transcript files is that they are stored as readable and executable PASCAL programs. A sophisticated end-user can edit the program to insert conditionals, iterations, and so forth. In certain situations, it is easier and quicker to create a script by programming than by demonstrating the actions to the algorithm animation system. Sophisticated users of the popular EMACS [68] text editor will note the analogy with tools for extending EMACS. At times, one may choose to create an EMACS macro by programming it in Mock Lisp. At other times, one chooses to instruct EMACS to transcribe a Mock Lisp program based on keystrokes and the current bindings of the keys, and then to edit the resulting file. At yet other times, one does not care how the macro is actually stored since one does not plan to edit it, just to use it.

4.2 Applications

We believe that scripts should be an integral part of idealized "electronic documents" of the future. A "conventional" electronic document would provide the framework for building "pages" and connecting them, traversing them, and so on. But within a page, at a place where there might be a static diagram in a book, there would be a script. The script would present information that the viewer could customize, and also would allow viewers the opportunity to interact with the underlying model. In the case of an electronic document concerning computer science algorithms, the underlying model would consist of algorithms, input generators, and views.

A scripting facility can serve as the basis for broadcasting one's screen to a network of workstations, and such a facility is an extremely useful vehicle for interactively demonstrating a system to others. The *broadcaster* acts as a script author and the *recipients* as script viewers. However, the transcript file is read by the recipients as it is being written by the broadcaster, not created on disk to be read later. Thus, any system that can store and replay transcripts can easily be extended to support broadcasting. For instances, in UNIX-like systems, the extension involves replacing calls to open and close a file with calls to access the appropriate socket. The actual calls to read or write the buffers comprising a transcript do not need to be changed. In an algorithm animation system, moreover, scripting and broadcasting are indistinguishable to client-programmers implementing algorithms, views, and input generators.

Figure 4.1 shows the relationship between scripting and broadcasting in detail. Figure 4.1(A) shows a script author in the process of creating a transcript file, and Figure 4.1(B) shows a script viewer in the process of replaying a script. Figure 4.1(C) shows the end-user making a transcript of his personalized playback. The transcript file he creates is not necessarily the same as the transcript file he viewed, since he can customize the playback. Figure 4.1(D) shows the end-user broadcasting a prepared script—with his customizations—to three recipients. In addition, one of the recipients is saving his own customized playback into a transcript file.

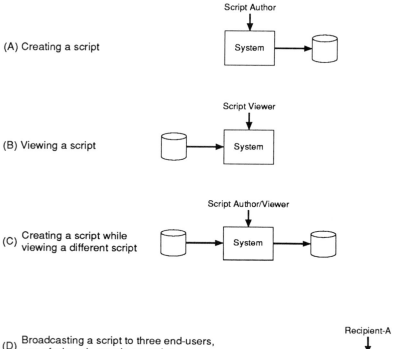

(A) Creating a script

(B) Viewing a script

(C) Creating a script while viewing a different script

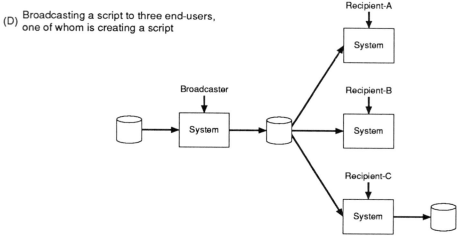

(D) Broadcasting a script to three end-users, one of whom is creating a script

Figure 4.1: *Relationship between scripting and broadcasting.*

Scripts can also function as extensible high-level macros. For example, when an algorithmatician is developing an algorithm and wants to run it through a series of tests, he can create a script by running the test once, and then simply rerun the script after each change to the algorithm. In addition, an end-user could edit the resulting transcript file so that a variety of algorithms are put through the same tests, or change the input data so that the test is more extensive than the sample run used to create the script. This strategy is particularly useful for debugging algorithms, views, and input generators, as well as for batch-oriented tasks such as creating images that require a long time to compute or render, and storing them on disk for hardcopy devices.

Another practical use for a scripting facility is to automatically maintain "research notes" detailing how some particular display happened to be created. Because a script involves little overhead, usually an unnoticeable pause as the end-user starts or resumes running an algorithm, it is feasible to keep a transcript always running. A running transcript file can be used to support a *redo* command. The redo would not reexecute the end-user's most recent command, but would reinstate the environment to its state when the algorithm began running. Analogously, an *undo* command could not revert each end-user action because, by design, each end-user action is not recorded in a transcript file. Only the changes in the state of the environment each time the end-user begins and resumes running the algorithm are recorded. Thus, an undo command would revert to the state of the environment at the point the end-user began making changes.

Finally, a yet unexplored use for transcripts is as a tool for self-instruction. We envision textbook exercises that would require students to determine what data must be given to an algorithm in order to achieve specific results. The system could check the student's arrangement of the environment state against answers stored in a transcript file.

4.3 Related Efforts

Previous research in electronic documents has not concerned making pages interactive or dynamic, but has concentrated on how parts of a document can be linked together to support nonsequential reading and writing. Nelson's Hypertext system is perhaps the best known, with its roots going back to Bush's 1945 Memex machine. There have been many implementations of primarily textual hypertext systems, from Engelbart's NLS in late '60s to Xerox PARC's Notecards in the mid-'80s. These systems, and others, have been well-documented in the literature [40]. Feiner's Electronic Document System [26] uses a high-resolution graphics picture rather than text as its notion of a page. Pages can best be thought of as nodes in a finite-state automaton, and they can contain animation sequences, created using an external animation language, as well as "buttons" to trigger arbitrary programs, including advancing to another page.

Recent systems such as Brown's Intermedia [73] have incorporated a variety of media, such as text, graphics, timelines, music, speech, and videodisks, into their notion of documents. Weyer and Borning's Electronic Encyclopedia system [72] uses a knowledge base to traverse the document and present the information; it is the only system that incorporates interactive simulations into documents. For example, an article about mirrors might contain a simulation in which the reader could place a variety of concave and convex mirrors of a specified curvature in the path of a laser light beam and see what happens to the path of the light. The Electronic Encyclopedia does not, however, support guided or customizable presentations of the simulations.

Our notion of maintaining the transcript file as an executable program is close in spirit to Halbert's SmallStar [33], a programming-by-example interface to a mockup of the Xerox Star office system.† In Halbert's system, an end-user's actions were recorded in a file and the system provided a readable representation of these sequential actions, with icons often representing data objects. Much of Halbert's research involved how a naive person could use a forms-oriented structured editor to add control structures and replace specific instantiations of data objects with more general descriptions.

Unlike SmallStar's designers, we can assume in designing our system that authors who wish to edit a transcript file in a non-trivial way have some computer sophistication. We have therefore chosen to record the transcript as an executable PASCAL program. This gives the author the complete generality of a programming language, which is not possible in SmallStar, but

---

† Readers unfamiliar with the Star can think of it as a precursor to the Macintosh Finder: objects are represented by icons and can be selected and moved. Dragging an object or set of objects onto another causes the latter object to operate on the dragged objects.

at the cost of needing to use PASCAL. Regardless of the author's sophistication as a PASCAL programmer, however, because the transcript is recorded as straight-line code with no flow of control and in a rather intuitively obvious manner, many unsophisticated authors can do a considerable amount of non-trivial editing of the transcript.

No other programming-by-example, programming-by-demonstration, and visual programming systems have influenced our work significantly. By and large, these systems are concerned with inferring a program by observing an end-user's actions, often involved with arranging icons. Even though both SmallStar and EMACS contain the notion of representing transcripts as editable executable programs, neither supports customizable playbacks.

Of the previous and current program visualization systems discussed in Chapter 2, only Movie/Stills by Bentley and Kernighan has some notion of scripts. In their system, an end-user user can build a sequence of animations using appropriate UNIX filters. For instance, different algorithm races can be created by merging different files together at the UNIX shell level. Such scripts are obviously not created by recording an end-user's actions.

4.4 The Author's User Interface

It is very simple for a script author to build a script: as an end-user, he issues the command to start the recording of his actions, and later issues another command to stop the recording. The algorithm animation system records not the author's keystrokes or commands, but rather the state of the algorithm animation environment—the structural, temporal, and presentation properties—when the author starts running the algorithms. Consequently, the author can experiment with changing the structural, temporal and presentation properties and the viewer will ultimately see only the properties in effect when the author began running the algorithms. While an algorithm is running, the author can control it like a regular end-user; he can stop it, resume it, and make all sorts of temporal and presentation changes. By default, the changes in the temporal and presentation properties are recorded in the transcript file each time the author resumes running the algorithms, but the author can override this default. The viewer can specify whether or not the author's temporal and presentation changes should be ignored.

BALSA–II provides script authors with some rudimentary facilities to allow viewers to synchronize the playback with written text or oral commentary. The FutureFreeze command causes the system to pause when it is replayed and also print a message. The FutureMessage command is like the FutureFreeze command except that it does not pause. This command is often used to echo input that the viewer would not normally see, report values of parameters, give descriptive information, or make annotations for virtually any reason. If the author does not want the current unit to be saved, he can issue a FlushUnit command. The author can abort the current running of the program using the Reset command. This command has no effect on the transcript file, but is useful as a shorthand to speed up the process of creating a script.

BALSA–II does not have any sophisticated tools for composing units into scenes and scenes into chapters. Each unit is stored in a separate transcript file, and a scene is a text file that lists the files containing the desired units. Similarly, a chapter is a file containing the names of the scenes and the names of the corresponding files.

There is much opportunity for research in tools for the script author. For instance, we envision a *script simulator* that would display an iconic representation of a script unit along a timeline. A new icon would be displayed at each change to the structural, temporal or presentation state. Double-clicking the icon would enlarge it so that the actual information concerning the state was visible and modifiable using textual and graphical editors. Marks induced by FutureFreeze and FutureMessage commands would be denoted visually along the timeline. Obviously, a script simulator could not know about the particular parameters or runtime-specifics without actually invoking the algorithms, input generators, or views.

4.5 The Viewer's User Interface

Figure 4.2 shows the table of contents of a typical chapter. An end-user begins viewing one of the scenes by double-clicking on its title or by selecting it and then the OK button. Scenes have textual names rather than icons because scenes within a chapter are usually related, making it difficult to create a unique identifying icon for each. After the last unit in the scene has been viewed, the dialog box in Figure 4.2 reappears with the next scene selected as the default.

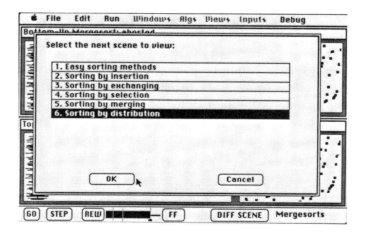

Figure 4.2: *Script viewer's control panel.*

Units within a scene have no associated labels, but are indicated by the marks on the horizontal bar in the control panel located in the bottom part of the screen in Figure 4.2. The spacing between the marks gives a rough indication of how much real time each unit takes to replay. The mark actually indicates the number of algorithm events that will be executed when the unit is replayed. As described in Chapter 3, the real time that each algorithm event consumes is a function of many factors. Fortunately, in practice, viewers are more interested in the displays than in checking their watches to determine how inaccurate the marks are.

The viewer can change units within a scene by dragging the rectangle on the slider-bar; the REW and FF buttons on the sides of the slider-bar are a shortcut for advancing to the next unit or returning to the previous unit. The DIFF SCENE button puts up the dialog box shown in Figure 4.2 and allows the viewer to change scenes and chapters. The GO and STEP buttons are the same as the normal interpreter functions found in the pull-down menus; they are provided in the control panel for convenience.

In addition to the commands located in the control panel, a viewer has access to all of the temporal and presentation commands normally available during execution of a program. The viewer can specify whether or not the script author's temporal or presentation changes recorded in the script should take effect on playback. Thus, the viewer has flexibility to use a script as a movie, by using the author's temporal and presentation changes, or just as a framework, ignoring the author's changes. Mixing the two styles must be done with some care, however, since the changes stored in a script may effect the changes being made by the end-user.

To the script viewer, the algorithm animation system is always in the "run" phase. Thus, he cannot change structural properties, such as the input generator, the algorithm, or their parameters. However, the viewer can suspend a script, terminate the algorithm that is currently running, thereby putting the system into a stable state, and then make the desired structural changes. A viewer might do this to rerun an algorithm with a new set of data, or with different algorithm parameters. When the viewer resumes playback of the script, the script continues with the unit following the one that had been executing when the playback was suspended.

As mentioned before, while an end-user is viewing a script, he can have the system record his personalized playback into a new script. This facility provides an easy way to make minor changes in a script. It also provides a record of a session that can be studied later or even adapted into a different script for other purposes.

4.6 Implementation Aspects

As we have seen, a script facility in an interactive system is used by different groups of people, each with different requirements and expectations. The goals of a script facility in an algorithm animation system are as follows:

- The transcript should contain information at a high level so that script authors can edit the transcript easily.

- Client-programmers should not be affected by a script. Neither animators coding views nor algorithmaticians coding algorithms and input generators should be concerned with scripts.

- The workstation environment underlying the algorithm animation system, not the systems guru implementing the algorithm animation system, should do most of the work necessary for creating and replaying transcripts.

This section examines the various tradeoffs to be considered in achieving these design goals and to what extent all of them can be achieved simultaneously.

First, consider what happens when an end-user hits a mouse button or a key on the keyboard. This is considered a *user event*—not to be confused with an algorithm event—and goes through the layers of software systems shown in Figure 4.3.

At the lowest level in the workstation environment (WSE), an event manager is responsible for generating a stream of user and non-user events. Typical non-user events are "update window W" or "disk inserted into drive D." There is typically software at an even lower level, but because that software is usually internal to the event manager, we do not consider it here. Above the event manager, but also part of the workstation environment, there is often a user interface management system (UIMS) which handles all input and feedback with the end-user. Whether or not there is a UIMS, the event is then processed by the algorithm animation system. Some user events, such as specifying parameters to algorithms, views, and input generators, are processed by the appropriate code implemented by the client-programmer rather than by the algorithm animation system.

As a general rule of thumb, the closer the package is to the "core of the

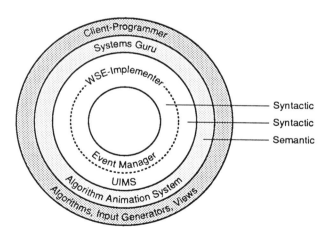

Figure 4.3: *Algorithm animation "onion."*

onion," the more microscopic is the nature of the information comprising an event. A transcript consisting of low-level events is typically verbose and difficult to read or edit. However, such a transcript has the advantage that it can be created and replayed without any change to the layers above it— other than issuing the command to specify the transcript file for reading or writing. Conversely, a transcript consisting of high-level events is easier to read and edit, but requires software at higher levels to implement the encoding and decoding of events.

The actions that an end-user performs to change the state of the environment are considered to be the *syntax* of a command, whereas the effect of the actions are its *semantics*. We now consider the implications of capturing events at these two levels.

Capturing Syntax

An algorithm animation system, like most interactive graphics applications, is structured as an event-driven process [2, 28]. The system waits for the next event to occur and then processes it. The following pseudocode illustrates this general schema:

```
repeat
    wait for next event from WSE
    process event
until exit
```

It is straightforward to modify this schema to process transcripts. To create a transcript, each end-user event must be encoded and appended to the transcript file. To replay a transcript, rather than obtaining the next end-user event from the event manager, a buffer is read from the transcript file and decoded into an end-user event. If the event manager is also used for non-end-user events, then these events must be processed as they are generated by the event manager, independent of whether or not a transcript is being used to generate an end-user event. The following pseudocode illustrates the basic schema for an event-driven application with a transcript:

```
repeat
  if event available from WSE then
    get next event from WSE
  else if reading from transcript then
    read the next buffer from the transcript file
    decode it as an event
  else
    wait for next event from WSE
  endif
  if writing to a transcript and event is a user event then
    encode the current event into a buffer
    append the buffer to the transcript file
  endif
  process event
until exit
```

The first call to the WSE is needed to process any non-end-user events that the event manager generates and to allow a script viewer to interact with the algorithm animation environment, including stopping the script reading. Note that this schema allows a transcript to be created while another is being read. The two transcripts will be identical except for any time stamps associated with the events.

Some workstation environments have integrated such transcript facilities into their event manager so that applications not even need be restructured. For example, applications written using the Macintosh toolkit can register a routine that is called by its *EventManager* to store bytes to a file, and another routine to read bytes from a file; however, storing and reading cannot be done simultaneously. This facility is used to create and replay "Guided Tour" diskettes, and is the basis for a number of commercial macro packages.

The advantage of recording events returned by the event manager, either by modifying the schema of the application, as we have suggested, or registering a function, as can be done with the Macintosh *EventManager*, is that transcripts are relatively transparent to the algorithm animation system and completely transparent to client-programmers. A drawback is that the size of the transcript file can grow very quickly, especially when mouse movement is recorded—as it usually is when a button is held down. A more serious shortcoming is that editing such a low-level journal in a non-trivial way is virtually impossible.

If the workstation environment has a UIMS, then the UIMS can be modified to capture the information at a higher level of abstraction than that provided by the event manager. In fact, because most UIMSs, by design, retain control of the main event loop, one cannot modify an application in a systematic way to handle transcripts; some support for transcripts must be provided in the UIMS.

If client-programmers also use the UIMS for interacting with end-users, then their code will also be correctly stored and retrieved in a transcript. The UIMS does not know whether it is being called by the algorithm animation system or by its clients, that is, the algorithms, input generators, and views.

The primary advantage to recording events at the UIMS level is that transcripts are relatively transparent to the algorithm animation system and code written by client-programmers. However, while the transcripts generated at the UIMS level are certainly more manageable than those generated at the event-manager level, they are still very large. A more serious problem with transcripts at the UIMS level is that they still capture just the syntax of the events. As a result, the playback necessarily shows all valid commands that the author issued; commands that cancel each other out, or make an incremental change to a previous command, cannot be detected at the syntactic level.

Figure 4.4 illustrates the difference between capturing the syntax of events at the event manager level and at the UIMS level. The fragment of the hypothetical transcript file shown in the figure corresponds to an end-user changing which view is inside a view window. The end-user first selected the view window by clicking the mouse while on that window, and then chose an entry from the appropriate menu. In the event manager transcript, the first two numbers in each line are the screen coordinates of the event, and the last number in each line is a flag indicating the status of the mouse (a four means the mouse button is depressed, a two means it is not depressed). The first three lines correspond to the end-user clicking in a window; the remaining lines correspond to the end-user depressing the mouse in the menu bar, and then lifting up on the button after it is on one of the choices, which happens to be located about 146 pixels below the menu bar. In the UIMS transcript, the location of the mouse click is recorded, followed by the name of the menu and the name of the choice within that menu.

Event Manager	UIMS
193,319,4	CLICK@(192,324)
194,319,4	MENU="View"/"Lson-Rbro Tree"
192,324,2	
118,16,4	
112,30,4	
103,62,4	
95,87,4	
104,101,4	
98,128,4	
96,149,4	
97,162,2	

Figure 4.4: *Fragments from a typical syntactic transcript file at the event manager and UIMS levels.*

Capturing Semantics

The semantics of an algorithm animation system or any other application cannot be captured by the underlying workstation environment because the workstation environment is, by design, independent of applications. Moreover, because the code that client-programmers write is independent of the algorithm animation system, even the algorithm animation system cannot capture the semantics of the client-programmer code. In practice, fortunately, this is not a serious problem, as we shall discuss below.

How do we capture the semantics? In an algorithm animation system, the semantics are the structural, temporal, and presentation states of the environment. It does not matter how the state got to its current configuration; what does matter is the state itself. The state can be changed in two situations. First, when the end-user changes from the "setup" to the "run" phase, the entire state must be recorded. Second, when the end-user resumes running the algorithms after he had temporarily stopped them, the difference between the state when the end-user stopped the algorithms and when he resumed them must be recorded. Both types of recording are straightforward and relatively concise. Figure 4.5 is an example of a transcript file containing semantic events.

As mentioned above, to a viewer, the difference between a script recorded at a syntactic level and one recorded at a semantic level is that the syntactic

```
AlgDef ALG=1 NAME='GrahamScan' PARMS='Shellsort'
InputDef ALG=1 NAME='FromFile' PARMS='d.x31.r100'
AlgWDef ALG=1 LOC=0., 0., 1., 1.  DRESSING
ViewWTiles 'H-SPLIT'
ViewWDef ALG=1 VIEW=1 NAME='Hull Details'
  + PARMS='' DX=0.  DY=0.  DZ=1.  NODRESSING
ViewWDef ALG=1 VIEW=2 NAME='Hull Only'
  + PARMS='' DX=.5 DY=.5 DZ=2.  DRESSING
Stops ALG=1 TryPt=1, 1, 5
Start
@127 DeleteView ALG=1 VIEW=2
@127 Freeze 'Let her rip now'
@127 Stops ALG=1 NewPt=0, 0, 5
@384 ViewWReloc ALG=1 VIEW=1 LOC=.5, 0., 1., 1.
@384 ViewWLoc ALG=1 VIEW=2 LOC=0., 0., .5, 1.
@384 ViewWDef ALG=1 VIEW=2 NAME='Classify Pts'
  + PARMS='COLOR' DX=0.  DY=0.  DZ=1.  NODRESSING
@593 Done
```

Figure 4.5: *A typical unit within a semantic transcript file.*

script is a virtual videotape of every valid command that the author issued; a semantic script shows the effects of meaningful commands only. If a virtual videotape is desired, it can be made automatically by low-level software, as mentioned previously.

To a script author who expects to edit a transcript file, the level at which the script is recorded is important. Semantic scripts are concise and more manageable than syntactic ones, and editing them is easier.

Effects on Client-Programmers

The last point to mention about scripts is their effect on client-programmer code. As will be discussed in detail in the next chapter, client-programmer code interfaces with end-users in four situations: parameters for algorithms, views, and input generators, and runtime specifics. This information provided by end-users in each of these situations must be stored into and retrieved from a transcript file.

In practice, most information that end-users specify is in the form of text strings or numeric values, choices among mutually exclusive options, or Boolean flags. This information is typically presented in the form of dialog boxes supported by the WSE, as shown in Chapter 3. The algorithm animation system provides an interface to the WSE's dialog package to store and retrieve the information. Thus, transcripts are transparent to the client-programmer.

However, when the end-user specifies information graphically, as by picking a node in a view of a graph, all that the algorithm animation system can do is to store and retrieve the coordinates of the mouse. While this is not a problem, it would be better for script authors to store a higher-level description of the pointing event in the transcript file. Hooks are available in our prototype algorithm animation system to do this; these are described in Chapter 6.

Transcript Format

The straightforward way to store the semantic information might produce a transcript of the sort shown in Figure 4.5. It reflects the following end-user actions. When the end-user began running the algorithm, the "setup" of the screen comprised a single algorithm window containing the GrahamScan convex hull algorithm. The parameter to this algorithm was the name of a sorting algorithm to use for preprocessing the points. The input generator was FromFile; its parameter was the name of the file it should process. The algorithm window filled the entire screen, its dressing was displayed, and it was tiled with two view windows: Hull Details and Hull Only. The second view window had its window dressing displayed, the image was enlarged to twice its original size, and the scrolling was such that the center portion of the image was centered in the view window. The only algorithm event that did not have its default step, stop and cost values was the event TryPt: its step flag was set, its stop value was 1, and it had a cost of 5. The end-user then began running the algorithm. When the event count reached 127, the script author deleted the Hull Only view, inserted a message for the script viewer, and removed the event TryPt as a stopping point. Later, when the event count reached 384, the script author created a second view window to display the Classify Pts view, and rearranged the location of the view window containing Hull Details.

It is easy to convert the transcript from Figure 4.5 into an executable program: edit each line textually and add some standard lines at the top and

```
#include 'ScriptDefs.h'

procedure Unit1;
  begin
  AlgDef(ALG1,'GrahamScan','Shellsort');
  InputDef(ALG1,'FromFile','d.x31.r100');
  AlgWDef(ALG1,0.,0.,1.,1.,true);
  ViewWTiles('H-SPLIT');
  ViewWDef(ALG1, VIEW1,'Hull Details','',0.,0.,1.,false);
  ViewWDef(ALG1, VIEW2,'Hull Only','',.5,.5,2.,true);
  Stops(ALG1, TryPt,1,1,5);
  Start();
  Time(127);
    DeleteView(ALG1, VIEW2);
    Freeze('Let her rip now');
    Stops(ALG1, NewPt,0,0,5);
  Time(384);
    ViewWReloc(ALG1, VIEW1,.5,0.,1.,1.);
    ViewWLoc(ALG1, VIEW2,0.,0.,.5,1.);
    ViewWDef(ALG1, VIEW2,'Classify Pts',
            'COLOR',0.,0.,1.,false);
  Done(593);
  end;
```

Figure 4.6: *The transcript from Figure 4.5, after some "syntactic sugar" has been applied, is now an executable* PASCAL *program.*

bottom. Such a transformation leads to the transcript shown in Figure 4.6.

Fortunately, with UNIX tools such as Lex and YACC, simple PASCAL interpreters are easy to build. Alternatively, and with much less effort, the transcript file could be run through the workstation's PASCAL compiler, and the executable version dynamically loaded when the end-user asks to run that script. In order to process such an executable program, the algorithm animation system must provide an entry point for each command that could appear in the transcript. To do that involves minor restructuring of the algorithm animation system: each command needs to be processed whether it is read as the first token in a line (e.g., "DeleteView..." in Figure 4.5) or as a routine (e.g., "DeleteView(...);" in Figure 4.6).

An even easier solution is possible: run the the program version of the transcript (Figure 4.6) to generate a text version (Figure 4.5). Each command that could possibly appear in the program version is a trivial procedure that merely outputs its arguments to a file. The structure of the algorithm animation system is a bit less complex when a transcript is read from a text file. A major limitation of this approach is that scripts cannot proceed conditionally based on end-user actions; the flow through the script is determined when the script starts up. A minor problem with this approach is that a script cannot be replayed immediately after it is created; the transcript file must first be compiled and then invoked to create its text version of the transcript. Actually, it is easy to replay a transcript immediately: as the program version is being created, also generate a second transcript file by invoking each command. This feature is needed when broadcasting is based on scripting.

4.7 Summary

In BALSA–I, we recorded the transcript at a syntactic level; this produced scripts that were limited to virtual videotapes and were very difficult to edit. In BALSA–II, we took the other approach: we stored transcripts at the semantic rather than the syntactic level. The effort required to support semantic transcripts in the algorithm animation system is well appreciated by script authors and script readers. By storing the semantics, end-users can customize the playback of both scripts and broadcasting, and can more easily edit the transcripts. However, it is still possible to introduce errors when the transcript file is edited; eliminating such problems, perhaps by using a "smart" script simulator, is an interesting research problem.

Using scripts as a basis for broadcasting raises a number of issues concerning synchronization. Each time the broadcaster polls the end-user (as happens frequently in an algorithm animation system, because the end-user is able to stop running the program at any time), the broadcasting machine must send a message to all recipients indicating that the end-user has been polled. In addition, the end-user's actions, if any, must also be transmitted. The problem with transmitting at each polling place is the load on the network. However, if the results of each poll are not transmitted, then recipients can execute ahead of the broadcaster. In addition, recipients will miss any temporal or presentation changes that the broadcaster makes.

The strategy adopted in BALSA–I was to allow the broadcaster to specify the frequency of transmitting synchronization markers. In addition, a synchronization signal was sent at each stoppoint the broadcaster had put in an algorithm. However, the synchronization was one-way: recipients would never get ahead of the broadcaster, but the broadcaster would not wait for any response from the recipients. BALSA–I adopted this one-way strategy to reduce network traffic. Network traffic was further reduced by broadcasting to only about one dozen nodes, and each of these nodes rebroadcasted to about five machines. Such a strategy would need to be extended if two-way synchronization were desired.

Rather than using scripts as the basis for broadcasting, it is possible to use tools provided by a number of contemporary workstations to display one end-user's screen (or even a specified window) to other end-users. Typically, such tools intercept the graphics display primitives on the broadcaster's workstation and transmit the primitives to a server running on each recipient's machine. Primarily because of the size of the graphics display file, such systems do not perform well in practice on current hardware. Even if performance were acceptable, we believe that using such built-in tools is not prudent because it is easy to extend scripts to include broadcasting. Moreover, only if broadcasting is based on semantic scripts can each recipient customize and personalize his display; broadcasting graphics primitives produce virtual videotapes.

In summary, we have found scripts to be an important aspect of an algorithm animation system and have consequently devoted much attention to their design, implementation and underlying model. We believe that the model can be used in a wide-variety of other interactive systems, since many can be characterized by structural, temporal, and presentation properties. For instance, the properties of a programming environment are very similar to those of an algorithm animation environment, whereas a spread sheet environment contains only structural and presentation properties. Unfortunately, however, it is still too difficult to program and edit scripts. Much research can be done on tools for authors, and on integrating scripts with current research on electronic documents. In particular, CD-ROMs create many new possibilities and challenges [45]; scripts are an approach that can exploit this technology for truly dynamic forms of communication.

5

Programmer Interface

This chapter describes the interface that our prototype algorithm animation system presents to client-programmers. Recall from Chapter 1 that there are two types of client-programmers: algorithmaticians who implement the algorithms as well as the input generators that provide data for the algorithms to manipulate, and animators who implement the graphical displays. Because the client-programmers' interface is molded by our desire to make algorithms appear to the end-user as interactive entities, readers of this chapter should be familiar with the nature of the prototype system's interactive environment described in Chapters 3 and 4.

The goals for the design of the client-programmers' interface are summarized as follows:

- *Independent Components.* Code for algorithms, input generators, and views should be separate and independent. An algorithmatician should be able to focus on the algorithm while completely ignoring the code required for its animation. An animator should be able to concentrate on implementing the animated graphic display while completely ignoring the nature of the algorithms that might be used to drive the animation.

- *Minimal Modifications.* Changes made in an algorithm for animation should have minimal effect to the algorithm proper. All modifications should be denoted conspicuously, so that after the algorithm has been prepared for animation, it can easily be returned to its original state.

- *Reusable Components.* Once an algorithm, input generator, or view is implemented, its interface should be frozen and become part of a library of such components. Adding, changing, or deleting an algorithm, input generator, or view from the library should not affect existing components.

Moreover, it should be possible to use any particular view to display aspects of itself, other views, or multiple aspects of the same algorithm.

- *Easy Implementation.* Creation of a new algorithm, input generator, or view should be quick and easy.

- *Real-time Performance.* Animations must happen in real-time. Any overhead and structuring necessitated by the algorithm animation system must have minimal impact on the runtime performance.

This chapter contains a considerable amount of terminology that helps make discussions more precise than otherwise possible. The examples presented in this chapter use simple algorithms, inputs, and views so the reader can concentrate on how pieces fit together. Animating a more complex algorithm, or designing a fancier view follows the same model.

Concerning the Examples

Examples are presented in PASCAL, although virtually any procedural language could be used. We assume a number of minor extensions to the language in order to improve readability of the examples. These extensions, which are commonly found in commercial PASCAL compilers, are as follows:

- The **module** statement indicates a block that can be compiled separately. Top-level entry points in it are external identifiers and are therefore available to all other routines, including the algorithm animation system. The structure of a **module** is the same as that of a **program**, except there is no "mainline."

- External files containing **const**, **type**, and external procedure, function, and variable declarations can be integrated into a module using the optional "**imports** *fn*" part of a **module** statement. The module can also contain its own **const** and **type** statements; local definitions override those found in any external files.

- Procedure, function, and module names can contain embedded periods. The periods have no semantic meaning; they are used solely for documentation.

- A function can return to its caller using a "**return** *val*" statement.

Finally, we assume two features of module blocks that are not commonly available. First, modules blocks can be nested and entry points in the nested block remain external identifiers. Second, modules blocks are reentrant. These features can be added to standard compilers by filtering modules through a preprocessor before compilation. Details are given in Chapter 6.

5.1 Algorithms

Our first step toward animating an algorithm involves making it appear to be more interactive to end-users. To do this, we introduce the notion of a structured algorithm, the algorithm we wish to animate modified in certain ways:

▶ *A structured algorithm is an algorithm that has been separated into subroutines to handle the algorithm code and the algorithm parameters; it also has subroutines to handle initialization and termination. The subroutines are called by the algorithm animation system; they do not call each other but communicate by shared global data.* ◀

A skeleton of a structured algorithm is shown in Figure 5.1. As indicated in the figure caption, all subroutines except the one to handle the gist of the algorithm are optional. A typical structured algorithm, such as the one shown in Figure 5.2, often contains only the mandatory subroutine.

In an unstructured algorithm, the end-user would be prompted to specify information relating to algorithm parameters at some point while the algorithm runs. In a structured algorithm, the code that interacts with end-users for specifying algorithm parameters is broken out into its own subroutine. Consequently, the algorithm animation system can let an end-user specify, change, and review this information when the end-user wants, not when the algorithm wants.

Placing initialization and termination code into separate subroutines does not represent any fundamental change in interacting with algorithms, as algorithm parameters do. Rather, they help improve real-time performance: garbage collection is not free, virtual memory is limited, and disk access is time-consuming. When an algorithm is run repeatedly, the algorithm can take advantage of the fact that it used some resources previously.

The *Code* subroutine of a structured algorithm is annotated to indicate the operations taking place within the algorithm. Annotations are also used

module *Alg.BTree*;

    var *global variables, including any "algorithm parameters"*

    procedure *Alg.BTree.Create*;
        This subroutine is called by the algorithm animation system exactly once, before any of the other subroutines are called.
    begin end;

    procedure *Alg.BTree.Dispose*;
        This subroutine is called by the algorithm animation system exactly once, after all of the other subroutines are called.
    begin end;

    procedure *Alg.BTree.StartRun*;
        This subroutine is called by the algorithm animation system each time the end-user issues a run command.
    begin end;

    procedure *Alg.BTree.EndRun*;
        This subroutine is called by the algorithm animation system after each time the B-Tree algorithm has finished running.
    begin end;

    procedure *Alg.BTree.Parms*;
        This subroutine is called by the algorithm animation system each time the end-user wants to observe or change the "algorithm parameters" for the B-Tree algorithm.
    begin end;

    procedure *Alg.BTree.Code*;
        Finally! Here is what one intuitively thinks of as "The Algorithm," after all extraneous statements have been removed. This subroutine is called by the algorithm animation system whenever the end-user issues a run command. It is preceded by a call to the ... StartRun subroutine and followed by a call to the ... EndRun subroutine.
    begin end;

    end.

Figure 5.1: *Code skeleton of a structured algorithm for building a B-Tree. All subroutines except the one to handle the essence of the algorithm (in this example, Alg.BTree.Code) are optional.*

to indicate when and what type of data the algorithm needs. Annotating an algorithms is a fundamental part of our model; the process is formalized as follows:

▶ *An annotated algorithm is a structured algorithm in which additional markers indicate phenomena to be of interest when the algorithm runs. These markers, called algorithm events, appear only in an algorithm's Code routine. Algorithm output events describe some segment of algorithm code. Algorithm input events describe what type of data an algorithm needs.* ◀

Figure 5.2 shows a structured and annotated version of Insertion sort. The algorithm output events are denoted by the procedure call *OutputEvent.xxx*, and input events by the function call *InputEvent.yyy*, where xxx and yyy are the event names. These routines are created by the algorithm animation system when the client-programmer defines the events, and their calling sequences are declared in the imported file.

An algorithm event has a name and a collection of parameters that provide additional information concerning the interesting phenomena in the program. Parameters to output events are read-only, whereas parameters to input events can be read-only, read-write, or write-only.

An output event causes each view to be notified with appropriate parameters to update itself. The algorithm is not concerned with what, if anything, happens in the graphical displays. Similarly, an input event causes the input generator to be notified with appropriate parameters to return appropriate information in the **var** parameters. Each input event also returns a flag indicating whether the logical end of file was reached. The algorithm is not concerned with how the input generator computes the information, or what constitutes the logical end of file.

The semantics of an algorithm event depends on the algorithm but should be used consistently in similar algorithms. For example, the event named *Swap* can be used both for sorting algorithms and for memory allocation algorithms, with very different meanings and syntax. However, all memory allocation algorithms should use the event *Swap* to mean the same thing. The intuitive notion of similar algorithms is formalized as follows:

▶ *An event dictionary is a collection of algorithm events. An algorithm's repertoire are those algorithm events with which it is annotated. Algorithms with the same repertoire are said to be functionally equivalent.* ◀

```
module Alg.Insertionsort imports 'InternalSorts.Defs';
  procedure Alg.Insertionsort.Code;
    var i, j, v : Integer;
        a : array[1 .. MaxN] of Integer;
        eofFg : Boolean;
    begin
    eofFg := InputEvent.HowManyKeys(N);
    for i := 1 to N do
      eofFg := InputEvent.ReadKey(a[i]);
    for i := 1 to N do
      OuptutEvent.NewKey(i, a[i]);
    for i := 2 to N do
      begin
      v := a[i]; j := i;
      while a[j − 1] > v do
        begin
        a[j] := a[j − 1]; j := j − 1; OutputEvent.Swap(j, j + 1)
        end;
      a[j] := v
      end
    end;
  end.
```

Figure 5.2: *Structured and annotated Insertion sort algorithm. Careful examination will reveal the algorithm preforming "set value" operations, but the algorithmatician has annotated the code as if they were "exchanges." The algorithmatician has such flexibility.*

Functionally equivalent algorithms can be interchanged and can use the same collection of input generators and views. In addition, they often share ancillary functions such as those pertaining to initialization and termination.

When an annotated algorithm runs, it produces a sequence of input and output events. We call the output events with their parameters an *algorithm trace*. The views on the screen can be thought of as an imaging of the algorithm trace. Thus, to the algorithm animation system and to the displays, it does not matter in what language the algorithm was coded, or if the events correspond to anything meaningful in the algorithm, or even if the events are being generated at random.

A practical use for an algorithm trace is to animate a complex algorithm that runs too slowly to produce real-time animations. An algorithm trace would be created off-line, say on a supercomputer, and then accessed by the workstation to give a real-time animation. Obviously, in such a situation, end-users would not be able to change any algorithm parameters or the data the algorithm processes; they could, however, interact with the displays. Other uses for algorithm traces can be found in Chapter 2 in the discussion of execution traces.

Animating an Algorithm

Animating an algorithm that uses an existing repertoire involves two steps: structuring the algorithm and annotating it with event markers. A previously structured and annotated functionally equivalent algorithm can serve as a prototype. If, however, the algorithm is sufficiently different from previously animated algorithms, then one must first define the algorithm events it needs.

In practice, structuring an algorithm involves little work, because the subroutines other than the *Code* subroutine are optional. In fact, structuring an algorithm may well reduce the total effort for algorithmaticians: because "extraneous" code is removed, it becomes easier to concentrate on the heart of the algorithm and to share ancillary functions.

Annotating an algorithm is also straightforward once its repertoire has been defined: the input events typically replace the system-specific input statements (e.g., *Readln*) and the output events replace the system-specific output statements (e.g., *Writeln*). Moreover, one could legitimately contend that algorithms are better implemented by replacing system-specific input and output statements with event annotations—even if no algorithm animation is involved—because event annotations provide a flexible interface to the outside. By default, an external package could be linked with the algorithm to print the name of each event and its parameters. More interestingly, different external packages could be linked with the same algorithm for different uses. One such package might perform statistical analysis on the distribution of events. Another package might generate static pictures of one or more data structures.

Algorithm Events

Just as there is no right or wrong way to break a program into subroutines, so there is no right or wrong set of algorithm events that constitute an algorithm's repertoire. The repertoire encapsulates the operations and data requests of an algorithm. What constitutes an operation depends primarily on what is intended to be displayed, which, in turn, often depends on the intended use of the animations. The events constituting a repertoire does indeed affect both end-users and client-programmers.

For end-users, the repertoire defines the level of abstraction they see. For example, suppose that instead of a single event with an array of N polygons as its parameter, there were N events, each with a single polygon as its parameter. Users would then encounter multiple events, instead of a single event, that they could use for stepping, stopping, and so on. This is more or less desirable depending on the intended use of the animation. Artificially biased comparisons may result if algorithms that are run together use different repertoires.

For client-programmers, the choice of events often influences their coding style. Algorithm events are independent of the data structures used in the implementation of the algorithms, input generators, and views; however, using data structures that are significantly different from those used by events may necessitate costly data conversion.

5.2 Input Generators

Associated with each algorithm window on the screen is an input generator selected by the end-user. The input generator provides data for the algorithm to manipulate, and a way for the end-user to control what data is provided. When an executing algorithm needs data, the request goes to the attached input generator. The algorithm animation system takes care of routing the request; the algorithm does not know which input generator is currently selected by the end-user.

Consider, for example, a sorting algorithm that reads N, followed by N numbers. An input generator might return a permutation of 1 through N, a collection of N (pseudo-)random numbers in some range, or an increasing sequence of N numbers; or it might read numbers from a file, generate them by a random number generator, or allow a user to specify them one at a time.

Input generators are not limited to textual interactions with users. Effective graphics-oriented interactions are possible, as illustrated in Chapter 3.

Input generators communicate with views in order to correlate what object(s) on the screen an end-user has selected. The communication process is analogous to the way algorithms use input events to request information from an input generator. However, in the case of an input generator requesting information from a view, the mechanism is through *correlate messages* rather than input events. There is also a mechanism analogous to output events, called *update messages*, that are used internally by views.

Messages and events are similar in the sense that they allow one procedure to call another procedure without knowing who the callee is; the algorithm animation system takes care of the routing. However, the difference between messages and events is more than nomenclature: end-users are aware of events, but not of messages. Events provide the abstraction of the algorithm through which the interpreter is controlled, whereas messages are an internal mechanism that allows inputs generators and parts of views to communicate.

Figure 5.3 shows the high-level relationship among an algorithm, input generator, and five views. The views have an internal structure not shown in the diagram. The internal structure is discussed in the next section.

Basic Concepts

The primary purpose of an input generator is to provide data to algorithms by responding to input events in the algorithm. Like algorithms, input generators are built as collections of routines each of which handles a particular function. Together these form an input generator with the following structure:

▶ *A structured input generator consists of a collection of routines that communicate by shared global data. The only required routines are the Data routines; they respond to algorithm input events. Other routines handle input generator parameters, initialization, and termination.* ◀

This structure parallels that of algorithms and enhances efficiency (because initialization and terminations routines are separated) and interactiveness (because the code to handle the input generator parameters is separated). Moreover, all code relating to the input generator's parameters is external to the structured algorithm.

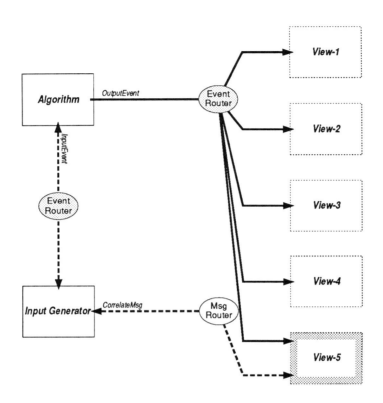

Figure 5.3: *The relationship among an algorithm, input generator, and five views at a high level. The notation, similar to that of Figure 1.2, is as follows. Boxes represent components implemented by client-programmers; the view boxes are dotted to emphasize that their implementation consists of a number of interacting components that are not shown. Ovals represent parts of the algorithm animation system that route information among components. Shaded ovals route events and unshaded ovals route messages. The solid paths indicate unidirectional flow of information, and the dashed paths indicate bidirectional flow. The view corresponding to the view window having the keyboard focus is highlighted.*

Figure 5.4 shows an input generator, *Input.SetOfKeys*, with its "standard" subroutines for input generator parameters, initialization and termination. This input generator can be used with the Insertion sort algorithm from Figure 5.2, or any other algorithm using the events defined in *InternalSorts.Defs*. Thus, an input generator, like an algorithm, has an interface by which it is characterized. This interface is as follows:

▶ *An input generator is characterized by a repertoire consisting of those input events to which it responds and those correlate messages it generates to the views. Input generators with the same repertoire can be interchanged without affecting any algorithms or views.* ◀

The more interesting routines of an input generator are the collection of *Data* routines that respond to each algorithm input event. By convention, the suffix of the *Data* routine is the name of the event to which it responds. Thus, if an algorithm uses the input event *yyy*, the algorithm contains the statement *InputEvent.yyy(...)*, and the input generator has a corresponding entry *Input.zzz.yyy(...)*, where *zzz* is the name of the input module. The calling sequences are identical. The top two subroutines in Figure 5.5 shows the routines for the input generator *Input.SetOfKeys* that handle the input events found in *Alg.Insertionsort*. (The third subroutines is discussed below.)

Not all information items that an algorithm needs can be specified by end-users before the algorithm starts running. The different types of information items are as follows:

▶ *Input generator parameters are information items provided by end-users before the algorithm starts to run. Runtime specifics are information items provided while the algorithm is running. End-users are prompted for runtime specifics as the result of an input event.* ◀

A practical difference between these types of inputs is that input generator parameters are independent of the graphical displays of the program since there are no views of an algorithm before it starts running, whereas runtime specifics are not necessarily so. Therefore, runtime specifics can allow end-users to specify information by pointing in a view window. This leads to the following description of how a point in a view window is given semantic meaning:

▶ *Runtime specifics can be textual or graphical. Semantic interpretation of graphical input, such as selecting one or more graphical entities, is done* module *Input.SetOfKeys* imports 'InternalSorts.Defs';

var N : *Integer*;   { parameter: how many numbers in the set }
        range : *Integer*;   { parameter: range of number generated }
        ct : *Integer*;   { how many have been generated already }

procedure *Input.SetOfKeys.Create*;
        This subroutine is called by the algorithm animation system
        exactly once, before any of the other subroutines are called.
    begin $N := 50$; *range* := *MaxInt* **end**;

procedure *Input.SetOfKeys.Dispose*;
        This subroutine is called by the algorithm animation system
        exactly once, after all of the other subroutines are called.
    begin end;

procedure *Input.SetOfKeys.StartRun*;
        This subroutine is called by the algorithm animation system each time
        the end-user issues the command to start running the attached algorithm.
    begin *ct* := 0 **end**;

procedure *Input.SetOfKeys.EndRun*;
        This subroutine is called by the algorithm animation system
        after each time the attached algorithm has finished running.
    begin end;

procedure *Input.SetOfKeys.Parms*;
        This subroutine is called by the algorithm animation system each time
        the end-user wants to observe or change the input model parameters.
    var *tmp* : *Integer*;
    begin
    Writeln('Current set size = ', N);
    Write('Enter new set size:');
    Readln(*tmp*); **if** *tmp* > 0 **then** N := *tmp*;
    Writeln('Current range is 0 through ', *range* $-$ 1);
    Write('Enter new range:');
    Readln(*tmp*); **if** *tmp* > 0 **then** *range* := *tmp*
    end;

Figure 5.4: *The "standard" subroutines of structured input generator Input.SetOfKeys. The subroutines shown in Figure 5.5 form the remainder of this module.*

function *Input.SetOfKeys.Data.HowManyKeys*
  (**var** *numPts* : *Integer*) : *Boolean*;
      This routine is called by the algorithm animation system
      after the input event HowManyKeys in the algorithm.
  begin
  numPts := *N*;
  return false   { no logical EOF for this event }
  end;

function *Input.SetOfKeys.Data.ReadKey*(**var** *v* : *Real*) : *Boolean*;
      This routine is called by the algorithm animation system
      after the input event ReadKey in the algorithm.
  begin
  v := (*Random* **mod** range);
  ct := *ct* + 1;
  return (*ct* > *N*)   { "has logical EOF been reached?" }
  end;

function *Input.SetOfKeys.Data.PickKey*(**var** *k* : *Integer*) : *Boolean*;
      This routine is called by the algorithm animation system
      after the input event PickKey in the algorithm.
  var *x, y* : *Integer*;
  begin
  Writeln('Please select a key from any view');
  WaitForDown;
  ReadMouse(*x, y*);
  return *CorrelateMsg.WhichKey*(*k, x, y*)
  end;

Figure 5.5: *The collection of Data routines for input generator Input.SetOfKeys from Figure 5.4. The routines here (from top to bottom) respond to algorithm input events HowManyKeys, ReadKey, and PickKey.*

by the display routine responsible for maintaining the image. The input generator communicates with that routine through correlate messages. ◄

The bottom subroutine in Figure 5.5 shows how the input generator *Input.SetOfKeys* responds to the algorithm input event *PickKey(key: Integer)*: by using a runtime specific to select a previously defined element. This runtime specific is graphical; an end-user would specify a key by pointing in a view window with the mouse. The correlate message, indicated by the function call *CorrelateMsg.WhichKey*, causes the algorithm animation system to call the view under the mouse with the specified parameters. That view takes the window coordinates (variables x and y) and correlates them to a key (variable k) among those it is displaying. The correlate message returns a flag indicating whether or not the end-user was pointing at a valid object.

When an algorithm runs, its only communication with the input generator is through input events. Just as we could drive the animated displays by feeding it an algorithm trace, we have the notion of an *input generator trace*: the stream of input events and their parameters that an input generator returns to an algorithm. The input generator trace is useful for independently debugging algorithms and input generators.

5.3 Views

This section introduces the basic concepts relating to views. Many of the concepts parallel those relating to algorithms and input generators. We will treat the similar aspects briefly and concentrate on those aspects that are peculiar to views.

Recall from Chapter 3 that each view window on the screen contains a view of the algorithm chosen by the end-user from a list of potential views. At any given time, the end-user can change which view is displayed in any particular window, create a new window or change the size and location of a window. The user can zoom and scroll through any view, and can tune the characteristics of each view through its parameters. A dominating theme of this thesis is the desirability of defining the views and the system in such a way that the animator implementing a view need only code the particulars of the view; all window-management aspects, for example, are handled by the system. Moreover, because views are complex to implement (even with a reasonable graphics environment), an algorithm animation system must allow views to be shared by many diverse algorithms.

Each view has three primary tasks:

- A view must be able to update itself incrementally each time an algorithm event occurs. Updates must be done in real-time.

- A view must be able to redisplay itself completely in an arbitrarily sized rectangular window using its internal data structures. This allows efficient implementation of zooming and panning, and opening a new view or changing what view is displayed in a particular view window while an algorithm is running.

- A view must be able to map coordinates from the screen into the objects that it displays, in response to correlation messages from the input generator.

None of these three tasks are absolutes; end-users will, however, notice the effects of any missing functionality. For example, if a view cannot map coordinates—either because the feature was not implemented or because selecting objects is not meaningful in the view—users will not be able to point at objects in that view in response to runtime specifics; the view can still be used, however, for displaying an algorithm's behavior.

To portray an image on the screen, we follow a classical computer graphics paradigm of a *modeler* and an *renderer*. The modeler creates and maintains a *model*, an abstract representation of the information that the renderer draws on the view window. The model is based, to a first approximation, on the output events generated by the algorithms. There might be many renderers for a particular model, simultaneously displaying different views in different view windows. Where we differ from traditional graphics techniques is in the way that modelers can be composed to display views of views, including themselves, or of multiple aspects of the same algorithm, and arranged hierarchically. This follows the spirit of composing UNIX programs by connecting filters together; we will elaborate on this analogy later in this chapter.

The reason we split the modeler from the renderer is efficiency: the modeler performs the expensive storage or computation aspects of maintaining and updating the model which is then drawn on the screen by the renderer.

Multiple renderers—either multiple instantiations of the same view or different, but similar, views—can use the same modeler. Thus, only a single model needs to be maintained for multiple views on the screen.

Because the information in the stream of output events generated by an algorithm does not necessarily correspond to the information the modeler and the renderer need, we introduce the notion of an *adapter* used to transform the data to the appropriate repertoire. The adapter allows views to be composed in interesting ways and to be reused extensively, as mentioned above.

Basic Concepts

A view is perceived very differently by end-users and by client-programmers (in particular, the animators implementing the view). To the end-user, a view is neither composable nor decomposable; it is chosen from a fixed list of possible views and is seen in a view window on the screen. To the animator, a view is composed of different parts handling specific things. These parts are as follows:

▶ *A view is composed of three parts: an adapter, modeler, and renderer.* ◀

▶ *A modeler computes a model based on update messages. The update messages that the modeler uses is called its repertoire. Modelers that use the same repertoire are said to be functionally equivalent.* ◀

▶ *A renderer draws an image of the model computed by the modeler onto a view window on the screen. It also maps a position on the screen into parts of the model. The renderer uses the same repertoire as does its modeler. In general, there are many renderers associated with each modeler. Renderers that share a modeler are said to be functionally equivalent; renderers that use different but functionally equivalent modelers are said to be functionally similar.* ◀

▶ *An adapter converts algorithm output events (from the algorithms) and correlate messages (from input generators) into corresponding update messages and correlate messages in the modeler and renderer's repertoire. Functionally equivalent modelers and renderers can share adapters. A separate adapter is needed for each group of functionally equivalent algorithms and input generators.* ◀

Once the modeler and renderer for a view have been implemented, their interface is frozen. To use it, an adapter must be written for each group of functionally equivalent algorithms in which one would like to use the modeler and renderer. The algorithm code is also frozen; adding a new view requires implementing an adapter, not modifying the algorithm. In practice, adapters are relatively easy to code. Many merely pass the incoming events to outgoing messages. (In BALSA–I, a modeler corresponded to a *vdsm*, and a renderer to a *view*. There was no concept of an adapter between the algorithm and the view, nor of attaching modelers to other modelers, as will be discussed later. As a result, views were not reusable in different domains of algorithms.)

Figure 5.6 shows how the views might be structured internally in a situation where there are five view windows on the screen. The image in each view window is drawn by one of the renderers. From this diagram, we cannot tell whether renderers Renderer–1 and Renderer–2 are the same view or are similar views that happen to share modeler Modeler–1. Likewise, we cannot say anything about Renderer–4 and Renderer–5, other than the fact that they follow the same repertoire as Modeler–3 and render an image of the model that Modeler–3 maintains. Modelers Modeler–1 and Modeler–2 use the same adapter Adapter–1; thus, their views, rendered by Renderer–1, Renderer–2, and Renderer–3, are all functionally equivalent.

Adapters, modelers, and renderers are structured, much like algorithms and input generators, into collections of subroutines that handle particular functions. The following definitions give the structure of each:

▶ A *structured adapter contains subroutines to handle* updates (*converting algorithm output events to view update messages*) *and* correlates (*converting from input generators to view correlate messages*). *In addition, there are routines to handle* initialization *and* termination. *These routines communicate by shared global data, and are optional.* ◀

▶ A *structured modeler contains subroutines to handle* updates, initialization *and* termination. *These routines communicate by shared global data, and are optional. Subroutines to handle* updates *maintain the model that is to be rendered.* ◀

▶ A *structured renderer contains subroutines to handle* updates, correlates, refresh, parameters, did, initialization *and* termination. *These routines communicate by shared global data, and are optional. They can access the*

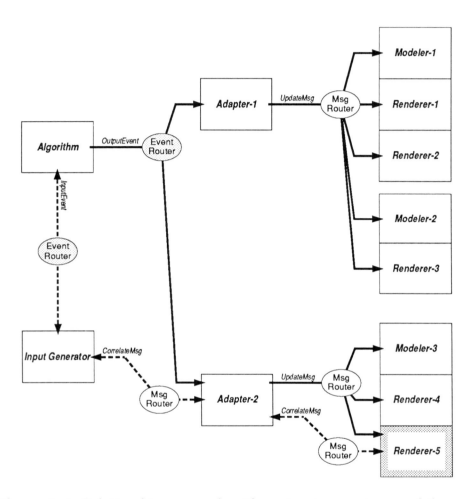

Figure 5.6: *Relationship among algorithms, input generators, and the components of a view. Compare this diagram to Figure 5.3.*

data structures maintained by the modeler, but cannot modify that data. The updates render the incremental modifications to the model; the correlates convert coordinates on the screen into objects of the model; the refresh routine renders the entire model; the parameters routine handles the view parameters analogously to the way that algorithm and input model parameters are maintained; and the did routine generates a device-independent description of the model into a file. ◄

The unique aspect of structured modelers and renderers lies in the way they interrelate. This relationship is illustrated in the high-level code skeleton in Figure 5.7 and graphically in Figure 5.8. Here there are two renderers that use it the same model. The end-user would see this as two potential views: one generated by *Renderer.R1* and the other by *Renderer.R2*. Of course, there may be any number of instantiations of the two views on the screen. Unfortunately, the PASCAL code does not tell the whole story. The algorithm animation system takes advantage of the fact the each module block is reentrant by allocating one instantiation of each renderer module for each view window on the screen. However, there will always be at most one instantiation of the modeler module. There is an instantiation of the modeler only when one of the view windows on the screen is generated by a modeler's renderer.

In certain circumstances, it is advisable to let a renderer maintain the model: for example, when a modeler supports a single renderer and it is anticipated that at most one instantiation of the renderer will be on the screen at any given time. A modeler would also be unnecessary if the data structures needed for maintaining the model are insignificant in terms of computation time or space.

Using Existing Views

Using a view that has already been implemented is straightforward. The animator merely implements an adapter that converts output events generated by the algorithm into the update messages for the view's modeler and renderer, and that converts correlate messages generated by the input model into correlate messages for the view's renderer. Once the adapter is written, all views whose modelers are functionally equivalent can also be used.

Consider how we might utilize the **Sticks** view from Chapter 3 to display the value of the array elements in Insertion sort shown in Figure 5.2, and

```
module Views.M;

    var variables comprising "The Model"

    module Modeler.M;
        These subroutines access and update "The Model"
        var variables for modeler M
        ...
        procedure Modeler.M.Update.xxx; begin ... end;
    end.

    module Renderer.R1;
        These subroutines access, but do not update, "The Model"
        var variables for renderer R1
        ...
        procedure Renderer.R1.Update.xxx; begin ... end;
        procedure Renderer.R1.Correlate.yyy; begin ... end;
        procedure Renderer.R1.Parms; begin ... end;
        procedure Renderer.R1.DID(fp : FilePtr); begin ... end;
        procedure Renderer.R1.Refresh; begin ... end;
    end.

    module Renderer.R2;
        These subroutines access, but do not update, "The Model"
        var variables for renderer R2
        ...
        procedure Renderer.R2.Update.xxx; begin ... end;
        procedure Renderer.R2.Correlate.yyy; begin ... end;
        procedure Renderer.R2.Parms; begin ... end;
        procedure Renderer.R2.DID(fp : FilePtr); begin ... end;
        procedure Renderer.R2.Refresh; begin ... end;
    end.

end.
```

Figure 5.7: *Schematic skeleton showing the relationship of two renderers based on the same modeler. The routines removed by the ellipses are the "standard" initialization and termination routines: ... Create, ... Dispose, ... StartRun, and ... EndRun. The ... Update.xxx routines refers to a collection of routines corresponding to the repertoire of update messages; similarly, ... Correlate.yyy correspond to the repertoire of correlate messages.*

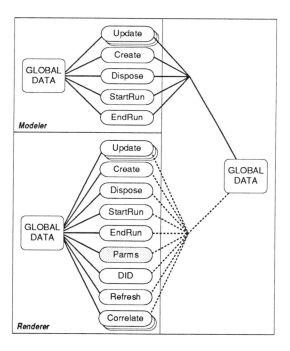

Figure 5.8: *A graphical representation of the modeler and renderer modules. The notation is as follows: each rectangle corresponds to a module, and the global data for the module is displayed. Each subroutine is shown as a flattened oval; the collection of routines for Update and Correlate are shown as the stack of flattened ovals. Solid lines indicate data that can be accessed and modified, whereas the dashed lines indicate a read-only access path. Subroutines that interact with end-users are shaded.*

the input generator shown in Figures 5.4 and 5.5. The **Sticks** view is part of a collection of views of an abstract object called a *Sequence*. In the example algorithm and input generator, a sequence would be a simple mapping to the array used in the algorithm. The table in Figure 5.9 shows the part of the *Sequence* repertoire that the **Sticks** view uses.

The version of the **Sticks** view shown in Chapter 3 is more complex than the one we are now describing. It has more entries in its repertoire in order to show comparisons, specially designated elements, and so on. However,

Message	Formal Parms	Description
WhichValue	*x, y: Integer* **var** *elt: Integer* **var** *val: Real*	If an element of the sequence were drawn at the specified screen coordinates, which element would it be and what would be its value.
SetName	*i: Integer* *name: String*	The *i*th element of the sequence has the specified label.
SetValue	*i: Integer* *v: Real*	The value of the *i*th element of the sequence is set to the specified value, a real number between 0 and 1.
ChangeValue	*i: Integer* *v: Real*	The value of the *i*th element is changed to the specified value, a real number between 0 and 1.
SwapElts	*i, j: Integer*	Exchange the values and labels of the *i*th and *j*th elements.

Figure 5.9: *Repertoire of messages used by the* **Sticks** *view. The entries above the dotted line are correlate messages, and those below the dotted line are update messages. It is assumed that all elements of the sequence will be defined using either SetName or SetValue before any ChangeValue or SwapElts occur.*

the basic ideas are the same as in the simplified repertoire shown.

The adapter consists of entry points to handle the two possible algorithm output events, *SetValue* and *SwapValues*, and one to handle the correlate message *WhichKey*. Because the abstract model generated by these output events is essentially the same as the abstract model described by the *Sequence* repertoire in Figure 5.9 it is not surprising that the adapter, shown in Figure 5.10, is quite simple. However, it is important to note that by using an adapter, the algorithms, input generators, can all be coded using conventions they each find most suitable without being influenced by any of the components with which they will eventually interact.

```
module InternalSort2Seq
  imports 'InternalSorts.Defs','Seq.Defs';

  function InternalSort2Seq.Correlate.WhichKey(
      var k : Integer;
      x, y : Integer) :
      Boolean;
    var v : Real;
    begin
    return CorrelateMsg.WhichValue(x, y, k, v)
    end;

  procedure InternalSort2Seq.Update.NewKey(k, v : Integer);
    begin
    UpdateMsg.SetName(k, Chr(Ord('A') + k − 1));
    UpdateMsg.SetValue(k, Real(v))
    end;

  procedure InternalSort2Seq.Update.Swap(a, b : Integer);
    begin
    UpdateMsg.SwapValues(a, b)
    end;

end.
```

Figure 5.10: *Adapter to convert from Insertion sort's output events and its input generator's correlate messages into the Sequence repertoire, expected by the* Sticks *view.*

Implementing a View

We now consider how the **Sticks** view is actually implemented. It is implemented by a renderer called *Renderer.Seq.Sticks* and uses a modeler called *Modeler.Seq*. The primary data structure of the modeler is an array of floating-point elements. It is maintained in the obvious manner based on the four update messages. The renderer would probably not need any data structures of its own, since the layout of the array is straightforward. In response to the update message *SetValue*, it sets a window into the world coordinate system for the graphics package (to be described later in this chapter) based on the number of elements defined so far as well as the minimum and maximum values. In response to the update message *SwapElts*, it simultaneously erases the sticks at the two positions and draws the new values. It would use the modeling package, described later in this chapter, for drawing and animating the sticks.

Another renderer that could use the same modeler, and also would not need any data structures of its own, is one that draws the elements of the sequence as dots, such as that shown in Chapter 3. Alternatively, one could just add a view parameter to *Renderer.Seq.Sticks* that indicates whether or not the full stick should be drawn or just the top of it.

Submodels

Continuing with the example from the previous section, consider a renderer that displays the modeler's array as an inversion table. That is, for each element, a stick is drawn whose height is proportional to the number of preceding elements larger than it. Computing the inversion table is relatively costly: an array either must be maintained with the inversion count for each element, or it must be computed dynamically in response to each change of a value. Who should maintain this array or compute the values dynamically?

If the renderer maintains the array, the problem is that multiple views of the inversion table (created by the end-user) will cause multiple arrays to be allocated and maintained. Yet if the modeler maintains the inversion table array, then the array is maintained even if the end-user does not chose to see any views of the inversion table. The overhead of "just one extra array" is small; however, if each potential renderer added "just a bit" of extra computation or space to the modeler, real-time animation would not be feasible.

Our solution is to create a modeler whose sole purpose is to maintain the inversion table. This modeler also needs to access the array of values, or else it must maintain the array itself—an undesirable alternative. We call a modeler that uses another modeler a *submodeler*; it is updated by the algorithm animation system after the parent modeler is updated. This is formalized as follows:

▶ *A submodeler is a modeler that can access the data structures of a parent modeler. Submodelers may in turn also have submodelers.* ◀

A submodeler is similar to a renderer in the sense that both can read, but not modify, their associated modeler's data structures. When an update message occurs, the parent modeler is notified of the event first, and then submodelers are notified in a breadth-first manner. Because a submodeler is itself a modeler, renderers are associated with it, as well as potentially submodelers. The primary purpose of a submodeler is to help achieve the efficiency necessary for real-time animations. The modeler does the bulk of the work, and then the additional work needed for certain views is done in a submodeler.

The basic schema for the modelers, submodelers and renderers for the sticks and inversions tables is shown in Figure 5.11.

Chained Models

The scenario we have just described for displaying the inversion table can still be improved upon: the inversion table maintained by the submodeler is itself an array. Why not let the sequence views be used to display it, rather than creating new views? That is, the renderers *Renderer.InversionTable.Sticks* and *Renderer.Seq.Sticks* are essentially identical. Moreover, although only two renderers are shown in Figure 5.11, in practice there could be many more. The entire barrage of sequence views should be available for viewing the inversion table.

This leads to the notion of chaining modelers together in order to form a "view of a view:"

▶ *A modeler is annotated with update messages in the same way that an algorithm is annotated with output events. A chained modeler is a modeler based on update messages generated by another modeler.* ◀

```
module Views.Seq;
   var  { "The Model" }
      a : array[1 .. MaxN] of Integer;

   module Modeler.Seq;
      . . .
   end.
   module Renderer.Seq.Sticks;
      . . .
   end.
   module Renderer.Seq.Dots;
      . . .
   end.

   module View.InversionTable;
      var  { "The Submodel" }
         t : array [1 .. MaxN] of Integer;
      module Modeler.InversionTable;
         . . .
      end.
      module Renderer.InversionTable.Sticks;
         . . .
      end.
   end.

end.
```

Figure 5.11: *Code skeleton illustrating the relationship of submodelers.*

Technically, a modeler could also be annotated with correlate messages (in response to correlate messages it was processing) to allow a view associated with the chained modeler to be used to specify graphical runtime specifics. However, in practice, chaining provides views of views, not direct views of data structures, which are typically used for graphical runtime specifics.

Figure 5.12 shows all the pieces of the puzzle. One could think of the submodeler in the figure as a modeler which maintains the inversion table, and the chained modeler as the sequence modeler. Thus, the sequence modeler is being used to provide a view of itself. Recursion is limited because the

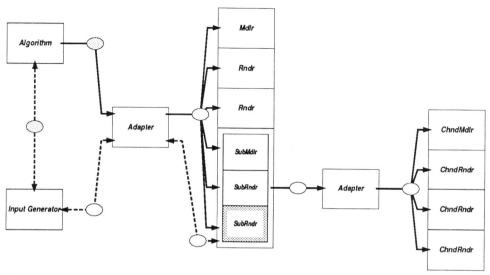

Figure 5.12: *Views using modelers, submodelers, and chained modelers.*

client-programmer defines for the algorithm animation system the relationship among the views.

5.4 Object-Oriented Pipes

Our model for structuring algorithms, input generators and views has been influenced in spirit by the concept of UNIX pipes and the object-oriented programming paradigm. We have found it helpful to think of the components that the client-programmer implements as "object-oriented pipes."

An algorithm functions like a UNIX filter: an algorithm transforms a stream of input events into a stream of output events. Each algorithm is independent of how the input stream was generated or of how the output stream is used, in the same way that a UNIX program is unconcerned with how data in *stdin* was generated or where data in *stdout* is going. In a shell notation, the idea is expressed as follows:

$$InputGenerator \mid Algorithm \mid View$$

However, standard one-dimensional, unidirectional UNIX pipes at the shell level are insufficient to describe how components communicate in an algorithm animation environment. Four problems are apparent. One, the input generator and the view need to communicate in order to support graphical runtime specifics; such communication is counter to the fundamental concept of shell pipes. Two, the input generator does not just generate data, but generates specific types of data based on requests from the algorithm; again, this communication is counter to basic shell programming concepts. Three, the shell has no syntax to describe splitting the output of one program into multiple filters, corresponding to the multiple views. Four, the interface between components is such that each component does not generate or expect a simple byte-stream. Rather, each component obeys a very particular repertoire.

Each component functions as an objects on two levels. Superficially, each component is an object with a well-defined set of routines. Figure 5.13 illustrates one possible way to view the relationships among the tasks each component must perform. Each node functions like a "class" in an object-oriented language, and the routines are the "methods" to which each class responds. Each class inherits the methods that its parent(s) have, in addition to possibly adding its own. In Figure 5.13, we see, for example, that class Algorithm is a subclass of End-User-Tuneable, which is a subclass of Module. The class Algorithm has methods *Code*, in addition to *Create*, *Dispose*, *StartRun*, *EndRun*, and *Parms*, which are inherited from the class End-User-Tuneable. The class Input Generator, because it is a subclass of End-User-Tuneable, shares with class Algorithm the fact that it responds to the methods *Create*, *Dispose*, *StartRun*, *EndRun*, and *Parms*.

The classes in Figure 5.13 are "virtual classes" in the sense that there will never be an instance of any of them and there will never be inheritance of the code implementing any of the methods. The relationship among the classes is the names of the methods to which they must respond, not the way in which they respond. Thus, "virtual classes" are quite different from, say, "abstract classes" in Smalltalk. In a Smalltalk abstract class, code is normally associated with each method, and the code is inherited (or overridden) by the subclasses.

Although we have shown the class Renderer with multiple inheritance, a subclassing hierarchy could be easily arranged. In fact, such a hierarchy might even be more appropriate because the methods *Update* and *Correlate*

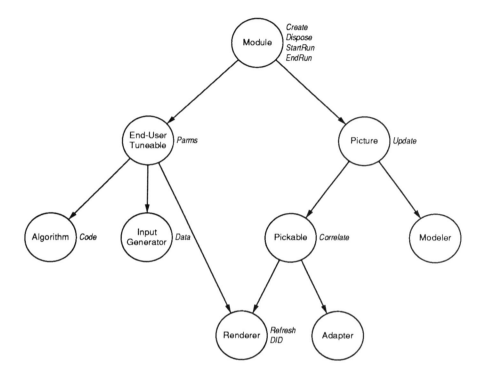

Figure 5.13: *Classes for Client-Programmer Components*

are used slightly differently by Renderers than by Adapters and Modelers: a Renderer cannot contain additional annotations in its response to *Update* and *Correlate*, but Adapters and Modelers can. However, the behavior of Adapter, Modelers and Renderers are close enough to justify the hierarchy we have shown.

The second way to view components as objects is aligned with conventional object-oriented programming styles. There are five abstract classes: Algorithm, InputGenerator, Adapter, Modeler, and Renderer. Each of these has its own hierarchy of abstract and non-abstract classes. For instance, Figure 5.14 illustrates the structure of part of the abstract class Algorithm. The leaves of the tree, displayed as squares, are the only non-abstract classes; they

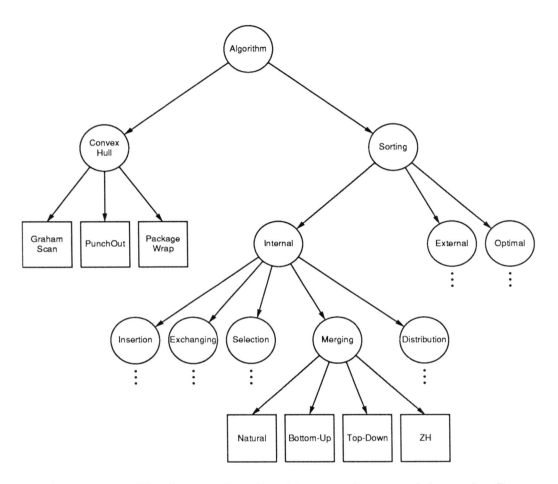

Figure 5.14: *The abstract class Algorithm contains two subclasses for Convex Hull and Sorting algorithms. The Sorting abstract class contains subclasses for internal, external, and optimal sorting methods, and the Internal sorting class contains subclasses for sorting by insertion, exchanging, selection, merging, and distribution. The Merging class contains non-abstract subclasses for four types of merge sorts.*

are the only classes of which there will be any instances. In fact, there would be one instance of a particular algorithm class for each algorithm window on the screen. It is reasonable to imagine that code is associated with each of the methods at any node above; the levels below a node would inherit the method or override the method with its own code. For example, all internal sorting algorithms might use an array for the elements being sorted which is initialized in the same way, say, with the largest value that can be represented. The merge-sorting algorithms then might override the internal sorting initialization with code to put each element of the array into its own subfile.

An important distinction of our components is that they are characterized by both incoming and outgoing events or messages. The class Algorithms, however, has only an outgoing repertoire, and the class Renderer has only an outgoing repertoire. Conventional object oriented languages, such Smalltalk objects, characterize objects solely on their incoming messages; no attempt is made to classify how objects behave on the basis of the other objects with which they communicate or the set of messages that they generate.

In the current implementation of BALSA–II, client-programmers use PAS-CAL, a non-object oriented language. Consequently, much of the object-oriented structure discussed in this section is derived by programmers following good software engineering practices. However, an algorithmic language with object-oriented support, such as C++ and Object Pascal, could provide this support more rigorously. Objects in these languages, however, do not support the notion of outgoing repertoires.

5.5 Graphics Environment

Each renderer displays an image in a view window on the screen. Although the end-user has a number of controls for manipulating the size and location of each view window and also for scrolling and zooming the image in the window, the renderer's code is not involved with any of this. It just draws into a window on the screen that it believes is stationary; the algorithm animation system, in conjunction with the underlying window manager on the underlying workstation environment (WSE), handles all interaction with the end-user. The WSE window manager clips all drawing primitives to the visible portions of each window. Everything works harmoniously—as long as the renderer is "well-behaved" and has a basic understanding of what is taking place behind the scenes. The remainder of this section describes what does take place.

The graphic primitives available to the renderer are provided by the WSE (e.g., QuickDraw in BALSA–II), and the primitives operate in pixel space. The essence of the graphics package (GP) provided by the algorithm animation system are entry points for the renderer to define a window-to-viewport transformation in the classical sense. The renderer sets a window—not be confused with a view window on the screen—onto the world coordinate (WC) system, and sets a viewport onto a normalized-device coordinate (NDC) system. For the moment, the reader should imagine that NDC space is differentially scaled to the entire drawing portion of a view window.

The renderer applies the transformation to each point directly. For example, the following three statements

$$GPwindow(0,0,70,40);$$
$$GPviewport(.5, .5, 1.0, 1.0);$$
$$DrawCircle(GPx(35),GPy(20), 10);$$

would cause a circle with a width of ten pixels to be drawn at the center of the upper right quadrant of the view window.

The graphics packages supports an additional transformation, often called a workstation window-to-viewport transformation, that maps a window onto NDC space into a viewport in device coordinates (DC). By convention, the workstation transformation is maintained by the algorithm animation system; the client-programmers do not use this transformation.

Consider the view shown in Figure 5.15. It contains a tree and a histogram indicating the number of internal and external nodes at each level in a slice at the right. The various coordinates transformations that takes place when the end-user zooms into the view and pans over it are illustrated in Figure 5.16. The client-programmer specifies the tree and the histogram in world coordinates; Window–1 in WC is mapped into Viewport–1 in NDC, and similarly Window–2 is mapped into Viewport–2. In Figure 5.16, these transformations are shown in thin dashed lines. To produce Figure 5.15, the default way the end-user would see the view, all of NDC space is mapped into the workstation's window manager window. In general, however, a portion of NDC space, the Workstation Window, is mapped into the Workstation

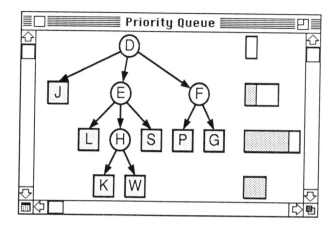

Figure 5.15: *Sample view drawn by a renderer. See Figure 5.16.*

Viewport, which is always set to fill the entire contents portion of the window manager's window.

The algorithm animation system changes the workstation transformation appropriately in response to end-user commands to increase or decrease the size of the view window, pan through its contents, zoom into its contents, or reframe the window. Only zooming and reframing can cause the size of the image to change; the other commands affect only where the image appears. In response to zooming or panning, the algorithm animation system also erases the entire window and calls the renderer to regenerate its entire image.

Renderers are typically designed to increase the level of detail when the image is sufficiently large (e.g., because the user zoomed into the view or the image was put into a large window), and to decrease the level of detail when the end-user is unable to see it. To find out what level of detail to use, the renderer can inquire the number of pixels separating each unit in world coordinates and also inquire the resolution of the output device.

The graphics package provides two additional facilities for renderers. First, screen coordinates can be converted into the renderer's world coordinate system, taking into account zooming, scrolling, and so forth. The renderer uses this facility when input generators need runtime-specifics that the end-user specifies by pointing to objects within a view window. The second

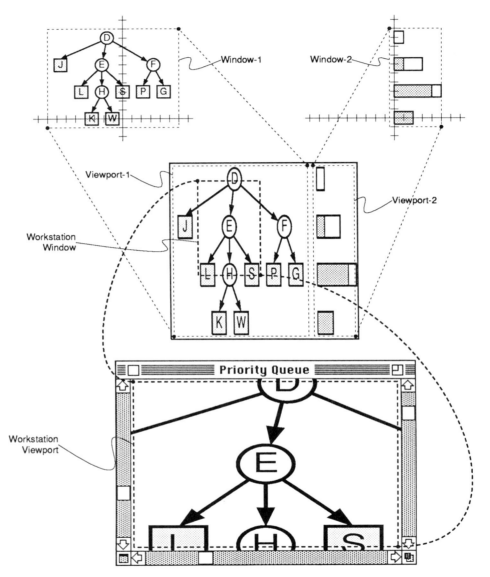

Figure 5.16: *Transformations supported by the algorithm animation system's graphics package. The window-to-viewport transformation is specified by the renderer, whereas the workstation window-to-viewport transformation, shown in bold, is specified by the algorithm animation system.*

function, a refresh, is used when the object being displayed by a renderer changes size. The algorithm animation system erases the entire window and calls the renderer to regenerate its entire image. Presumably, the renderer will have changed the window onto the world coordinate space to take into account the current size of the object. This allows a render to shrink or expand its drawing to fill the view window.

Simplicity

By design, the graphics package is extremely simple and efficient—the two transformations are collapsed into a single integer multiplication, division and addition—yet powerful. It is a hybrid package that allows animators to combine high-level specifications with low-level "pixel-tweaking" control.

Unlike traditional graphics packages, there is no concept of segmentation. Two primary reasons for segmentation are to do pick correlation and image regeneration. In our application, neither of these justify the overhead. First, because much end-user interaction is handled by special-purpose components, such as menu and dialog managers, pick correlation is needed only in response to runtime specifics. In practice, simple non-sophisticated methods for correlating objects to screen locations work well. Second, the renderer must be able to do image regeneration in order to allow end-users to change views while an algorithm is running or to create a new view window while the algorithm is in progress. The regeneration is based on the data structures maintained by the modeler.

Modeling Package

Not part of our prototype algorithm animation system per se is a modeling package that has been developed by animators. This package contains many of the fundamental routines that have been highly optimized, both aesthetically and computationally. For example, the Sticks view discussed above would use entries in the modeling package for, say, moving an overlay of a specified height from one stick to another. An algorithm animation system supports many different types of algorithms and displays. Making the modeling package part of the animators' domain gives animators more control over it. As more standard types of displays emerge, parts of the modeling package will most likely become part of the algorithm animation system.

6

Implementation

The purpose of this chapter is to present an overview of BALSA–II's internal structure and to summarize its interface to client-programmers. We do not aspire that this chapter serve as a manual for client-programmers or as documentation for the system. The treatment of the material is necessarily ununiform: novel aspects are described in detail and straightforward aspects are mentioned only superficially.

BALSA–II consists of two parts: a preprocessor and an application. Client-programmers invoke the BALSA–II *preprocessor* in lieu of a compiler; end-users are not aware of the preprocessor's existence. The preprocessor adds compile-time and execution-time support for code that client-programmers implement. Compile-time support includes creating definitions of events and messages as external entry points with appropriate arguments, and transforming modules so they are reentrant and can be nested. A standard compiler then compiles the transformed modules. Execution-time support involves building a program-readable database that captures the information provided by client-programmers about events, and relationships among algorithms, input generators and views.

End-users invoke the *application* part of BALSA–II and most likely think of it as "the algorithm animation system." As with any well-designed software system, its clients are not aware of its internal structure. End-users are concerned with the effects of each command available to them, whereas client-programmers are concerned with the specifications of information they provide.

This chapter is organized as follows: we first describe the preprocessor, then the application, and after that, the specifications of interest to client-programmers. We conclude by discussing portability issues and aspects of the design that are susceptible to attacks by malicious client-programmers.

6.1 The BALSA–II Preprocessor

The BALSA–II preprocessor can be thought of as an "implementation detail." A production-oriented algorithm animation environment would undoubtedly integrate the functionality of the preprocessor into a program development environment using bona fide databases, incremental compilers or interpreters, structured editors, and so on. However, for a prototype research-oriented system, a preprocessor provides desirable flexibility: it allows client-programmers to use existing and emerging programming environments, and to code using virtually any programming language that is program-callable with the algorithm animation system. Some aspects of the preprocessor are language-dependent, however, and must be modified for each language that client-programmer use. In particular, procedural languages with object-oriented support can be used for structuring algorithm, input generator, and view libraries. The BALSA–II design, as discussed in Chapter 5, is conducive to such a style.

The preprocessor facilitates portability and implementation of the algorithm animation system. For instance, rather than modifying a compiler or implementing one ourselves to support reentrant code, we use the preprocessor to make a textual transformation of the client-programmer's source code. The transformed code can then be compiled in the standard way. The drawback is that client-programmer's must strictly adhere to certain conventions. In a research-oriented prototype, this assumptions is reasonable.

The BALSA–II preprocessor is implemented as a collection of executable programs shown in Figure 6.1.

PreDict takes as input an event or message dictionary and generates three output files. The first file, *GlueRtns*, contains a collection of subroutines, one for each event and message in the dictionary. These subroutines, or glue routines, serve as an interface to the BALSA–II entry point that actually processes events and messages. More details concerning the nature of these routines are given below. The file routines is compiled and linked with the BALSA–II application. The second file, *Defs*, contains declarations of the event and message subroutines. There is an output file corresponding to each input dictionary file; it is imported by client-programmer modules in the **module** statement. The third file, *EventsDB*, is a program-readable version of information of interest to end-users about each event. For each event, it contains a label to refer to the event, and the default step, stop,

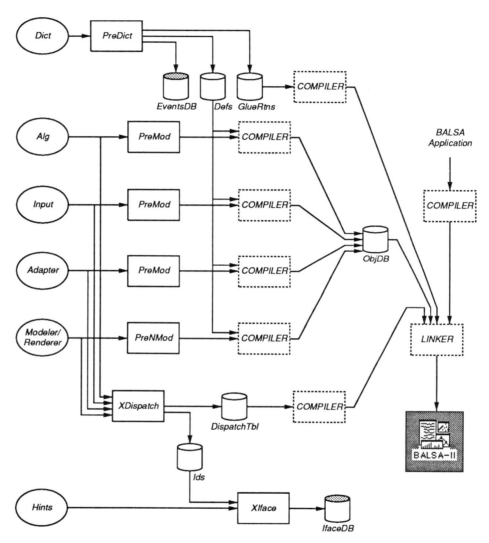

Figure 6.1: *The preprocessor. Ovals represent text files created by client-programmers; rectangles represent executable programs—those in dashes are compilers and linkers provided by the workstation environment; and the disk icons represent files created by the preprocessor. The shaded disks are accessed by BALSA–II at runtime.*

and cost values associated with the event. BALSA–II accesses this file at execution-time when end-users control the interpreter.

PreMod converts an algorithm, input generator, or adapter module implemented by a client-programmer into a module that is reentrant after it is compiled by a standard PASCAL compiler. *PreNMod* is similar to *PreMod*, but more complex because it transforms nested modules, i.e., modelers, renderers, and submodelers and their associated renderers. Nested modules must not only be made reentrant, but their entry points must be made callable from an outer scope, in particular, the one containing BALSA–II. Details concerning making modules reentrant and unnested are given below.

XDispatch determines the runtime address of the glue routines, the client-programmer modules, and the routines in each client-programmer module. It collects the names of all routines by scanning the modules and dictionaries, and assigns a unique integer identifier to each one. It then creates a lookup table, *DispatchTbl*, that BALSA–II uses at execution-time to determine the address of the procedure corresponding to a given identifier. The lookup table is compiled and linked with the BALSA–II application, at which time references in it are resolved. *XDispatch* operates at a lexical basis; it assumes that modules observe the naming conventions illustrated in Chapter 5.

XIface creates a program-readable file *IfaceDB* containing a description of client-programmer components and their intrarelationships. There are five types of relationships: (1) which components can be used with each other, e.g., which input generators are meaningful with which algorithms, which adapters to use in various situations; (2) the hierarchy of modelers, renderers, and submodelers; (3) which events are used by each algorithm; (4) the textual name presented in menus to end-users for identifying algorithms, input generators, and views; and (5) a way to figure out the purpose of each subroutine in each module, e.g., which is the *StartRun* subroutine and which the *Dispose*. The information needed to create *IfaceDB* is provided by the client-programmer in a *Hints* file.

Glue Routines

The purpose of the glue subroutine associated with each event or message is to collect the parameters to the event or message and then transfer control to BALSA–II, which calls the appropriate client-programmer subroutine(s) to process the event or message. Glue routines treat events and message in the same way; to simplify the discussion, we will limit the discussion to events.

Some care must be given to the glue routines because a subtle problem occurs when BALSA–II calls the client-programmer's subroutine to process the event: what calling sequence should be used? The calling sequence must set when BALSA–II is compiled, yet each subroutine expects to be called with its own calling sequence, corresponding to the parameters for the event it processes.

An efficient solution, but one that is system-dependent, is for the glue routine to determine the number of bytes its parameters occupy on the calling stack, and to call BALSA–II with three parameters: where the parameters are located on the calling stack, the number of bytes the parameters occupy, and which event has occurred. BALSA–II can setup the stack appropriately before it calls the client-programmer subroutine(s) to process the event. With some care, parameters need to be put on the calling stack only once regardless of the number of client-programmer modules that are notified of the event.

A portable, system-independent solution is for each event to be processed by a pair of glue routines. One routine would just take its calling arguments, put them into static global variables, and call BALSA–II identifying which event has occurred. BALSA–II would use the second glue routine instead of calling a client-programmer subroutine directly. The second glue routine would call the client-programmer's subroutine passing to it the static global variables it had previously saved.

Both of these strategies can be implemented automatically by lexically processing the information in an event dictionary.

Another detail that must be considered concerns duplicate event names. We restrict duplicate names to appearing in separate dictionaries. Thus, an event such as *Swap* in sorting algorithms could have a different calling sequence than *Swap* in memory allocation algorithms because they would be defined in different dictionaries. A solution is as follows: each event is assigned a unique name and the *Defs* file maps the name the client-programmer uses into the unique name.

Reentrant Modules

Recall that an end-user can have multiple copies of the same algorithm, input generator, or view on the screen simultaneously. Because each component is implemented as module, a collection of routines that share global data, a problem arises: how is each instantiation of a module given its own global data? That is, each module must be reentrant, yet PASCAL compilers, by and large, do not generate reentrant modules. Fortunately, the effect can be achieved using some relatively straightforward coding conventions.

An easy way to achieve reentrant modules is to dynamically load multiple copies of the desired module. Unfortunately, dynamic loading may or may not be efficient or even possible, depending on the underlying operating system. Moreover, loading multiple copies of the same module so that each module is given its own global data is often explicitly prohibited. Even if it is possible, dynamic loading multiple copies is an inefficient approach because only one copy of the code is really needed. Nested modules, used for submodelers and renderers, pose yet another difficulty because, in general, internal modules cannot be dynamically loaded.

An approach that we was not available to us in implementing BALSA–II is to run each instantiation of a module as a separate process. This approach, however, has its own set of complications concerning communication and synchronization. It raises a number of interesting research problems that we will touch upon in the next chapter.

A standard solution, independent of whether or not a module can be dynamically loaded or multiple processes are available, is to allocate data for each module and to pass each routine in the module the data on which it should operate. Thus, a module acts as an "object" in a classical object-oriented framework, and the routines in the module are its "methods."

We implement the standard solution with a minor variation: rather than passing data to each routine, each routine inquires of BALSA–II what data it should process. This variation facilitates nested reentrant modules, described below. A module can be transformed automatically by a simple lexical analysis of it. Figures 6.2 and 6.3 show the "before" and "after" versions of a sample module.

Let us now examine in detail the modifications *PreMod* made to the module in Figure 6.2 to derive the one shown in Figure 6.3. *PreMod* first groups the global variables for the module into a record and assigns it a unique datatype called *M.DataT*. It also creates routines, *M.DataTCreate* and *M.DataTDispose*, that allocate and deallocate a block of data of that type. A new instantiation of the module is created by calling *M.DataTCreate* to allocate a block of data and saving the returned pointer. The body of

```
module M;
  type Point = record who : Cardinal; horiz, vert : Real; end;
  var pts : array[1 .. 100] of Point; N : Integer;
  procedure M.StartRun;
    begin
    N := 0
    end;
  procedure M.Update.IdPt(pt : Integer; id : Cardinal; x, y : Real);
    begin
    pts[pt].who := id;
    pts[pt].horiz := x;
    pts[pt].vert := y
    end;
  ...
```

Figure 6.2: *A typical module as implemented by a client-programmer.*

each routine is prefaced by the following line:

with *M.DataTPtr↑(FindData)* **do begin**

The routine *FindData*, part of BALSA–II, returns a pointer to a data block previously created by a call to *M.DataTCreate*. Actually, *FindData* just returns a pointer to a byte in memory; the pointer must be typecast into a *M.DataTPtr* pointer. The code written in each routine does not need to be modified because the **with** statement ensures that all global variables actually refer to their current instantiations.

If the client-programmer's routine is "well-behaved"—and it will be unless the results of the preprocessor are modified— *FindData* knows which data to return: it is the data associated with the module containing the client-programmer subroutine most recently invoked by BALSA–II.

```
module M;

    type Point = record who : Cardinal; horiz, vert : Real; end;
    type M.DataT =
        record pts : array[1 .. 100] of Point; N : Integer; end;
    type M.DataTPtr = ↑MDataT;

    function M.DataTCreate : M.DataTPtr;
        var tmp : M.DataTPtr;
        begin
        New(tmp);
        return tmp
        end;

    procedure M.DataTDispose(tmp : M.DataTPtr);
        begin
        Dispose(tmp)
        end;

    procedure M.StartRun;
        begin
        with M.DataTPtr↑(FindData) do begin
        N := 0
        end
        end;

    procedure M.Update.IdPt(pt : Integer; id : Cardinal; x, y : Real);
        begin
        with M.DataTPtr↑(FindData) do begin
        pts[pt].who := id;
        pts[pt].horiz := x;
        pts[pt].vert := y
        end
        end;

    . . .
```

Figure 6.3: *The module from Figure 6.2 after support for reentrant modules has been added. The highlighted statments are inserted automatically by the BALSA–II preprocessor.*

Nested Modules

Two additional modifications are made to nested modules. First, nested modules must be made unnested, so that all subroutines in it appear in the outer scope. *PreNMod* moves the **type**, **const**, and **var** declarations to the outermost scope, and then removes the nested module's **module** and corresponding **end.** statements. Client-programmer must be aware that modules are no longer nested. In particular, routines that once took precedence over identically named routines may now conflict with those routines. In addition, shared internal routines may no longer be shared or internal. These limitations, in practice, are not major considerations; client-programmers seem to adapt without difficulty.

Second, renderers and submodelers need to access the data of their associated modeler in addition to their own data. *PreNMod* transforms each module as *PreMod* does, except the body of each routine is prefaced with an appropriate collection of **with** statements corresponding to its scoping levels.

Figure 6.4 shows the **with** statements that preface the body of a routine in a renderer associated with a submodeler. The modeler is called *Modeler.Hull*, the submodeler, *Modeler.ClassifyPts*, and its renderer is called *Renderer.ClassifyPts*. The routine *Renderer.ClassifyPts.Refresh* would be in the outer scope of the modeler. *FindData* is able to return pointers to the correct data blocks because, as part of BALSA–II, it has access to the hierarchy of modelers and renderers from the *IfaceDB* file.

```
procedure Renderer.ClassifyPts.Refresh; outermost scope
  var variables for this routine
  begin
    with Modeler.Hull.DataTPtr↑(FindData) do
    with Modeler.ClassifyPts.DataTPtr↑(FindData) do
    with Renderer.ClassifyPts.DataTPtr↑(FindData) do begin
    code for this suboutine
    end
  end;
```

Figure 6.4: *A typical routine in a nested reentrant module. The highlighted lines are inserted automatically by PreNMod.*

6.2 The BALSA–II Application

We describe the application part of BALSA–II in two parts: first we describe its primary data structures, and then we walk through its major subsystems. The description of the interpreter is considerably more detailed than the other subsystems; a working knowledge of its fundamental algorithms is useful for understanding the precise semantics of how multiple algorithms are synchronized and how the end-user controls their execution.

Data Structures

BALSA–II's primary data structures are categorized as follows.

World This data structure contains in-core information created by the preprocessor: *EventsDB*, *IfaceDB*, *DispatchTbl*, *GlueRtns* and *ObjDB*. The data structures corresponding to files *EventsDB* and *IfaceDB* are created by BALSA–II when it starts up and accessed in read-only mode thereafter; the data from *DispatchTbl*, *GlueRtns* and *ObjDB* are linked with the BALSA–II system and are also only accessed in read-only mode at run-time.

Mode A Boolean flag indicating whether the environment is in a stable or unstable state. Various commands, especially those affecting the structural properties, are only available to end-users when the system is stable. The environment is initially stable, and becomes unstable when algorithms begin to run. It returns to the stable state after all algorithms have completed—because they finished or the end-user terminated them.

Structural properties This data structure corresponds to the structural properties defined in Chapter 3. Structural properties include which algorithm is inside each algorithm window, which input generator has been selected, and the current values of the algorithm and input parameters.

Temporal properties This data structure corresponds to the temporal properties defined in Chapter 3. Temporal properties are each algorithm's current step, stop and cost values associated with each algorithm event.

Presentation properties This data structure corresponds to the presentation properities defined in Chapter 3. Presentation properties include the layout of algorithm and view windows, whether or not the window dressing should be displayed on each window, which view is inside each view window, and the view parameters for each view window.

Runtime properties This data structure contains four types of information for each algorithm: (1) The "data block" for each active module. The data block contains the global variables for each (reentrant) module. (2) The "environment" for each algorithm. As will be explained below, each algorithm is run as a coroutine. The environment consists of the stack that is allocated to each algorithm, and the current values of registers, including the program counter, stack pointer, and frame pointer. (3) For each algorithm event: the number of times it has occurred since the algorithm started running, the number of times it has occurred since the last time it caused a stop, and its current contribution to the algorithm's virtual time. (4) The amount of "idle" time remaining. The idle time is set to the cost of the most recent event. Each time the BALSA–II scheduler is ready to run the algorithm, it first decrements the idle time, and then runs the algorithm only if the idle time is non-positive.

Input Script A Boolean flag indicating if a script is currently being read. If so, this data structure includes a substantial amount of additional information such as what part of the script file has been processed, how many units comprise the current scene, and the scenes and chapter names comprising the script.

Output Script A Boolean flag indicating if a script is currently being written. If so, this data structure includes information concerning the file being written such as its name and a pointer to access the file.

Major Components

This section describes BALSA–II's major subsystems at a fairly high-level. The subsystems are shown in Figure 6.5, along with the code written by client-programmers. In the figure, an asterisk labeling a client-programmer module is a short-hand for all five of the types of components that client-programmers implement. The Interpreter subsystem is shown in more detail than the other subsystems; it contains routines *Runner*, *EvtRouter*, *MsgRouter*, and *Poller*.

Commander Subsystem

The Commander subsystem controls the action: after initializing data structures and various packages, it sits in loop calling routine *MainEvent* until the end-user exits the application. Routine *MainEvent* determines the next event from the WSE's event manager and processes it appropriately. It differs from standard Macintosh applications in three fundamental ways. First, BALSA–II supports two-levels of nested windows, whereas the Macintosh toolkit assumes no hierarchy of windows. Second, BALSA–II uses high-level scripts rather than the journaling feature of the Macintosh toolkit. Third, BALSA–II provides the illusion of multiple processes that can be interrupted (almost instantaneously) by the end-user. The Commander also contains an entry point called *AnyMainEvents*, that returns a flag indicating whether there exists any events available for *MainEvent* to process.

Although the Commander is called recursively from the Interpreter, there is no possibility for infinite recursion. In fact, the recursion is limited to a single depth: when the Interpreter is called by *MainEvent* recursively, it notices this fact because the global mode flag indicates the environment is unstable. The Interpreter merely returns, which in turn, causes *MainEvent* to return to its caller, the Interpreter. We will describe this process in more detail below when discussing the Interpreter subsystem.

Menu Subsystem

The Menu subsystem has three entry points. The first, *MenuInit* is called once, at the very beginning. The second, *MenuUpdate*, controls which menu choices are valid by examining the global data structures. It is called by the Commander at the beginning of *MainEvent* in order to invalidates those menu items that are not valid, and validates those that are. For example, when the system is unstable, end-users are not allowed to change which input generator to use. The third entry point in the Menu subsystem, *MenuEvent*,

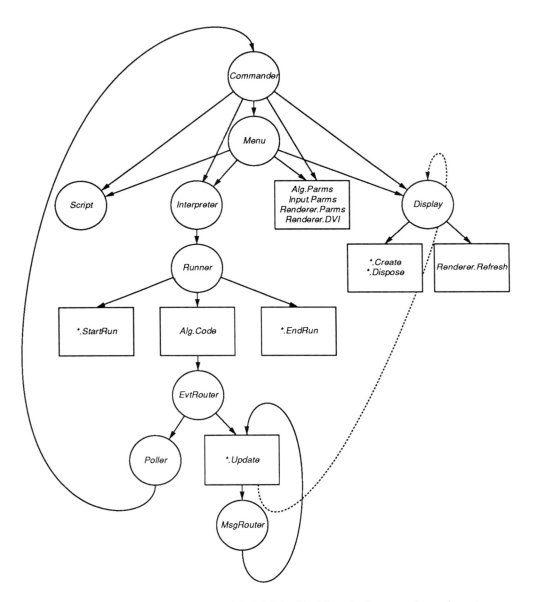

Figure 6.5: *Major subsystems of BALSA–II. The circles are the subsystems, and the rectangles are routines that client-programmer code.*

is invoked after the end-user has selected a menu item by pressing a "command key" or by selecting a choice from a pull-down menu. *MenuEvent* calls the appropriate routine to process the end-user's command.

Script Subsystem

The Script subsystem has three major tasks: create a transcript file, replay a transcript file, and handle the end-user commands available to script authors and script viewers. Many aspects of the implementation were described in Chapter 4; here we sketch briefly the processes of creating and replaying transcripts and how they are integrated into the remainder of the system.

While a transcript file is being created, the Commander calls the Script subsystem each time the end-user goes from the "setup" to the "run" phase. The appropriate Script entry compares the current structural, temporal, and presentation properties with its copy of those properties from the previous time it was called, and outputs to the transcript file those that are different.

To replay a transcript file, a temporary text transcript file is first generated from the PASCAL version of the script. Thereafter, *MainEvent* is responsible for processing the script: in addition to checking the WSE's event queue, it checks the transcript file to see whether the next line in it should be ignored, processed, or deferred. A line would be *ignored* if it contains a presentation change and the script viewer specified to ignore the script author's presentation changes on playback. A line would be *deferred* if it contains a change that should happen while in the "run" phase, but the specified event count has not been reached yet in the executing algorithm. Otherwise, the line is *processed* by invoking the appropriate routine.

Display Subsystem

The Display subsystem functions as a very high-level window manager: it is "very high-level" in the sense the the underlying workstation environment, the Macintosh Toolkit, provides a rich set of tools for manipulating the windows. Thus, the majority of the Display subsystem involves calling the appropriate Toolkit function in response to each end-user action. It contains some straightforward logic to effect the two-levels of window hierarchy that BALSA–II presents to end-users.

The Display subsystem also contains an entry, indicated by the dotted path in Figure 6.5, that a renderer's *Update* subroutine can invoke to cause the view window to be refreshed. As described in Chapter 5, the view window is refreshed by BALSA–II invoking the renderer's *Refresh* routine. Finally, the Display subsystem is responsible for maintaining the "workstation transformation" of the graphics package in response to end-user actions to size, move, pan, zoom, expand and reframe.

Figure 6.6 illustrates the relationship among the various routines that are responsible for the interactive graphics that end-users see. The renderer's *Update* subroutine generates images using a combination of the modeling package (MP), the algorithm animation system's graphics package (TGP), and the WSE's graphics primitives (QuickDraw). The *Parms* routines for the algorithm (A.P), input generator (I.P), and renderer (R.P), as well as an input generator's *Data* subroutine that interacts with end-users to processes runtime-specifics (I.D), use parts of the WSE's interaction toolkit, e.g., the *DialogManager* and the *ControlManager*. They do this through a layer provided by the algorithm animation system (DP) that handles storing or retrieving the information from a script file. These routines can also access the WSE's interaction toolkit and graphics primitives directly; however, when they do so, they must follow use the script hooks, described below.

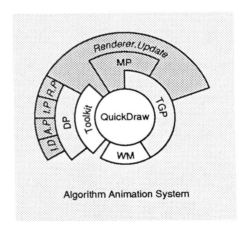

Figure 6.6: *Relationship among the algorithm animation system (light gray), client-programmer code (dark gray), and the workstation environment for interactive graphics (white).*

Interpreter Subsystem

The Interpreter subsystem, while not very large, is integral to the algorithm animation system. Consequently, we will describe it in more detail that we have described the other subsystems.

The interpreter calls each algorithm in a round-robin fashion, transferring control to the next algorithm after each algorithm event. Unbeknownst to the algorithm, each is called by the interpreter as a coroutine. The interpreter gets control back when the algorithm executes an output or input event. It executes the event by calling the input generator or view appropriately (details below), and then it "polls." Polling has three purposes: first, it allows the end-user to stop running the algorithms; second, the system checks whether executing the algorithm event has caused any pausing or stopping points to be reached; and third, it transfers control to the next algorithm that is ready.

The interpreter has five external entry points corresponding to the end-user's commands: Go, GoGo, Step, StepStep, and Reset. Each of the four "run" commands first sets a global flag to indicate which of the four styles has been specified and then calls procedure *Runner*. The best way to describe *Runner* is in an informal pseudocode:

Algorithm for *Runner* routine.

Step 1a. If the system is stable (and it will be the first time that *Runner* is called), create a circular list of active algorithms, initialize the runtime data structures for each algorithm, and finally invoke all modules' *StartRun* procedure. Continue at Step 2.

Step 1b. Otherwise, the system is unstable. Set an Interpreter global flag, called *resumeFg*, to be true and return. The effect of this return is that the *Poll* routine, which had previously called the Commander's *MainEvent* routine recursively, resumes.

Step 2. Set the global mode flag to be unstable.

Step 3. Transfer control to the next algorithm on the circular list of active algorithms. Control will eventually return to Step 4 after one of the algorithms has finished running, either because it came to its end or because the end-user issued the Reset command on the only non-terminated algorithm.

Step 4. Remove the algorithm that has finished from the circular list of active algorithms. If any algorithms remain on the list, continue at Step 3.

Step 5. Set the global mode flag to be stable and invoke all modules' *EndRun* procedure.

The *Poll* routine, called after each algorithm event has been executed, is also a bit tricky. We again resort to an informal pseudocode to explain its operation:

Algorithm for the *Poll* routine.

Step 1. Update the runtime information for the executing algorithm to reflect the event that occurred.

Step 2. If there are no events to be processed as determined by calling the Commander's *AnyMainEvents*, continue at Step 3. Otherwise, set the flag *resumeFg* to be false. Loop, calling the Commander's *MainEvent* routine recursively, until the *resumeFg* becomes true. When the *MainEvent* routine is called recursively, the system is in an unstable mode. Consequently, *MenuUpdate* allows the end-user to stop the algorithm and change only temporal and presentation aspects. The *resumeFg* is eventually set true because the end-user executed a Go, GoGo, Step, StepStep, or Reset command.

Step 3. Check the current algorithm event for interest. We say it is of *minor interest* if it is in the set of stepping events for the algorithm; it is of *major interest* if its stop value is positive and it has been executed that many times.

> *Step 3a.* If the event is of major interest and the end-user had issued either a StepStep or GoGo command, a *pause* is reached: display an appropriate message stating the event reached, and wait a moment to allow the end-user to read the message. Continue at Step 4.

> *Step 3b.* If the event is of major interest and the end-user had issued either a Step or Go command, a *stop* is reached.

> Similar to Step 2 above, repeatedly call the Commander's *MainEvent* recursively until the end-user issues a run command. Continue at Step 4.

Step 3c. If the event is of minor interest and the end-user had issued a StepStep command, a pause is reached. Proceed as described in Step 3a.

Step 3d. If the event is of minor interest and the end-user had issued a Step command, a stop is reached. Proceed as described in Step 3b.

Step 4. Loop through the circular list of algorithms (decrementing its "idle" time) until one is reached that is ready to resume running. Transfer control to that one.

The final entry point in the Interpreter subsystem corresponds to the Reset command: it removes the selected algorithm from the circular list of runable algorithms and, if there are no more algorithms in the list, it sets the *resumeFg* to be true.

The Interpreter subsystem is also responsible for routing events and messages. The internal functions to do this are called *EvtRouter* and *MsgRouter*, respectively, in Figure 6.5. Routing input events is easy: the appropriate function of the input generator is invoked with parameters corresponding to those in the algorithm input event. Routing output events is also easy: all of the appropriate adapters for active renders are invoked with parameters corresponding to those in the algorithm output event. Routing update messages generated by the adapters is more complex. The idea is to notify the update routines for all modelers, and then the update routines for the renderers. Care must be taken to ensure that sub modelers are invoked after their parent modeler(s). The order of notifying modelers and renderers is found by traversing the data structures comprising the temporal properties. Correlate messages are handled analogously. For efficiency, the routers can examine a module's repertoire to determine whether or not the module should be invoked for a particular event or message.

The message routing network in Figure 6.5 appears to be highly recursive, though, in fact, it is not at all. If the recursion were "unrolled," it would reveal each rectangular box to be a different instantiation of a (usually different) module. Figure 6.7 shows a different perspective of the routing process.

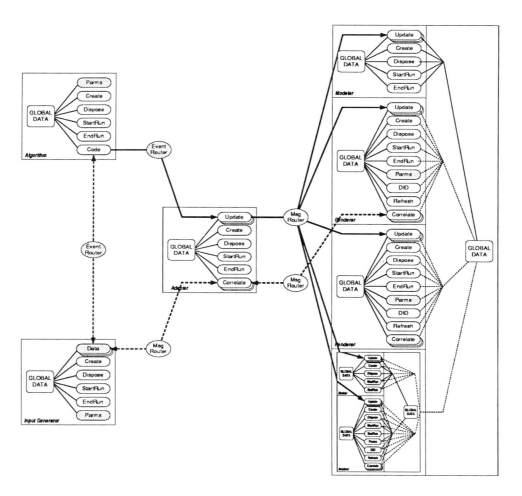

Figure 6.7: *The "big picture."*

The two occurrences of *EvtRouter* and the three occurrences of *MsgRouter* appeared as the highly "recursive" single instantiations in Figure 6.5.

6.3 Client-Programmer Specifications (Summary)

This section summarizes the various components that client-programmers implement. The information is necessarily brief; complete descriptions for most of the concepts can be found in Chapter 5.

Dictionaries

Client-programmers create two types of dictionaries: an *event dictionary* defining algorithm output and input events, and a *message dictionary* defining update and correlate messages. As described earlier in this chapter, the preprocesser generates three types of files from the information contained in a dictionary: glue subroutines to implement each event and message; definitions of the glue subroutines so client-programmer modules can use the routines; and information about the events in a format that can be accessed efficiently at runtime. Parameters to events and messages can be of user-defined data types: a file containing the declarations of the user-defined types can be imported by the file containing the glue routines, as well as by the client-programmer modules using events and messages. The following information is specified for each event in a dictionary:

Syntax The event name and its arguments. These must be valid PASCAL identifiers. Input events, but not output events, may specify **var** parameters.

Name A string representing the "name" that end-users see when referring to this event for setting step, stop, and cost values. The null string prevents an end-user from accessing any of these values.

Default Step Flag A Boolean flag indicating whether or not this event should be in the default set of events constituting a step. If the event name is the null string, then to be fair to end-users, the default step flag should be set false.

Default Stop Amount An integer indicating how many times this event should occur before it causes a stop point to be reached. If the event name is the null string, the default stop amount should be 0.

> *Default* An integer indicating the amount of time this event should
> *Cost* consume. If the event name is the null string, the default cost
> amount should be 0.

Because end-users are not aware of messages, only syntactic information
needs to be specified for each message. Update messages, but not correlate
messages, may use **var** parameters.

In essence, the dictionaries that a module uses defines its repertoire, and
determines which modules can be with each other and which can be interchanged.

Script Hooks

In Chapter 4, we mentioned that scripting is transparent to the client-
programmers as long as standard dialog boxes are used to interact with end-
users for obtaining information. Transparency is achieved because BALSA–
II provides a layer above the WSE's user interaction packages to handle
saving and retrieving the information to and from transcript files. This layer
was shown in Figure 6.6 as *DP*. However, when the client-programs use non-
standard types of interaction techniques, or when information is specified
by pointing at parts of the view, only low-level information can be recoded
automatically. While this does not present any problems functionally, it does
makes transcript files difficult to edit for a script author.

There are four types of subroutines that interact with end-users. The first
three, an algorithm's *Parms*, an input generator's *Parms*, and a renderer's
Parms, handle algorithm, input generator, and view parameters respectively.
The fourth, an input generator's *Data* subroutine, need only be considered
when it responds to an algorithm input event by prompting the end-user for
runtime-specifics.

Consider an algorithm's *Parms* routine. It is actually called by the algorithm animation system for four purposes. The most common reason why
the *Parms* routine is called is to interact with the end-user to examine and
modify the algorithm parameters. However, while an algorithm is running,
end-users can only view the parameters and cannot change them. The final
two reasons why the *Parms* routine is also called are to encode the parameters into a text buffer, and to decode the parameters from a previously
encoded text buffer.

An input generator's *Parms* routine is also called in the same four situations. However, a renderer's *Parms* routine always allows the end-user to change the parameters. That is, there is never a situation when temporal parameters cannot be modified by the end-user, whereas structural properties (i.e., algorithm and input generator parameters) can only be modified when the system is in a stable mode.

A *Parms* subroutine that by-passes the standard script processing (e.g., because it uses custom interaction techniques) has the following general schema:

```
if replaying script then
  decode parms from buffer
else
  if reviewing parms then
    display current parms, in read-only mode
  else
    display current parms, allowing end-user to
      modify, default, and cancel
  endif
endif
if writing transcript then
  encode current parms to buffer
endif
```

Entry points are available in BALSA–II to determine the reason why the subroutine was called. The subroutines to process view parameters and runtime specifics are never called in a "read-only" mode; thus, the second **if** statement is unnecessary.

The client-programmer has full control over what information appears in the transcript file; the animation system never looks at the contents of the buffer.

Components

Client-programmers implement five types of components: algorithms, input generators, adapters, modelers, and renderers. Each component contains subroutines invoked by the algorithm animation system to perform specific tasks. The following chart summarizes the tasks expected of each type of component:

Algorithm	Input Gen.	Adapter	Modeler	Renderer
Create	*Create*	*Create*	*Create*	*Create*
Dispose	*Dispose*	*Dispose*	*Dispose*	*Dispose*
StartRun	*StartRun*	*StartRun*	*StartRun*	*StartRun*
EndRun	*EndRun*	*EndRun*	*EndRun*	*EndRun*
Parms	*Parms*			*Parms*
Code *OutputEvent* *InputEvent*	<u>*Data*</u> *CorrelateMsg*	*Update* *UpdateMsg*	*Update* *UpdateMsg*	*Update*
		<u>*Correlate*</u> *CorrelateMsg*		<u>*Correlate*</u>
				Refresh
				DID

The annotations each task may utilize is shown in small typeface, and the annotations that return a Boolean flag are underlined.

All components perform tasks *Create*, *Dispose*, *StartRun*, and *EndRun*. The components with parameters that end-users can manipulate directly (i.e., algorithms, input generators, and renderers) perform the task *Parms*. Those that participate in building view images on the screen (i.e., adapters, modelers, and renderers) perform the task *Update*, and those involved in correlating a location from the view window on the screen to parts of the model being displayed (i.e., adapters and renderers) also perform the task *Correlate*. The relationship among the tasks is shown graphically in Figure 5.14.

Annotations

Events and messages are denoted by subroutine calls, whose name is determined by concatenating the type of annotation to the name of the event or message as it appears in the syntax part of the dictionary where it is defined. The names of the annotations are as follows: *OutputEvent, InputEvent, UpdateMsg,* or *CorrelateMsg.*

Input and output event annotations can only appear in an algorithm's *Code* subroutine, and update message annotations can only appear in the *Update* subroutine of an adapter or a modeler. Correlate message annotations can only appear in an input generator's *Data* subroutine or in an adapter's *Correlate* subroutine.

Input events return a Boolean flag indicating whether or not the data is valid. Correlate messages also return a Boolean flag; it indicates whether or not the data being correlated is valid. Output events do not return any information.

Module Formats

The remainder of this section shows the format of each module, first in PASCAL and then graphically.

Algorithm Module

```
module Alg;
   var ...;
   procedure Alg.Create; begin ... end;
   procedure Alg.Dispose; begin ... end;
   procedure Alg.StartRun; begin ... end;
   procedure Alg.EndRun; begin ... end;
   procedure Alg.Parms; begin ... end;
   procedure Alg.Code; begin ... end;
   end.
```

Figure 6.8: PASCAL *skeleton of an algorithm module.*

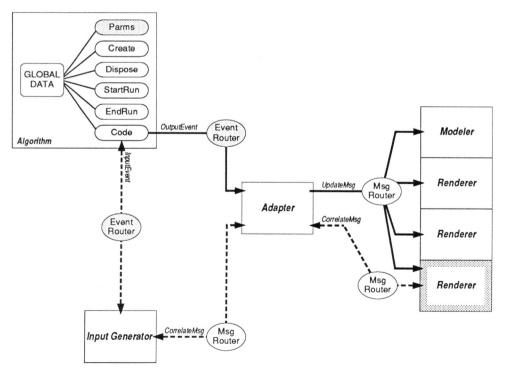

Figure 6.9: *Graphical representation of an algorithm module.*

Input Generator Module

There is one *Data* routine corresponding to each algorithm input event to which the input generator responds. It is shown in the PASCAL code as a single entry with the suffix *xxx*.

```
module Input;
    var ...;
    procedure Input.Create; begin ... end;
    procedure Input.Dispose; begin ... end;
    procedure Input.StartRun; begin ... end;
    procedure Input.EndRun; begin ... end;
    procedure Input.Parms; begin ... end;
    procedure Input.Data.xxx(...); begin ... end;
    end.
```

Figure 6.10: PASCAL *skeleton of an input generator module*

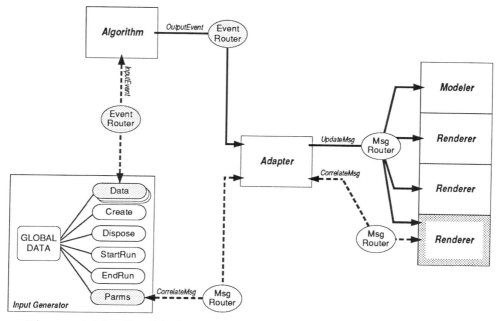

Figure 6.11: *Graphical representation of an input generator module.*

Adapter Module

Adapter modules convert output events from an algorithm into update messages for modelers and renderers, and correlate messages from an input model into correlate messages for modelers and renderers. An adapter can also be used as part of a chained modeler to provide "views of views." In this situation, rather than converting output events from an algorithm, it converts update messages from a modeler. The differences are transparent to the adapter. The two types of adapters are shown in the graphical representations.

An adapter contains a collection of *Update* and *Correlate* routines. Each collection is represented by a single entry with a suffix *xxx* or *yyy* in the PASCAL code skeleton.

```
module Adapter;
  var ...;
  procedure Adapter.Create; begin ... end;
  procedure Adapter.Dispose; begin ... end;
  procedure Adapter.StartRun; begin ... end;
  procedure Adapter.EndRun; begin ... end;
  procedure Adapter.Update.xxx(...); begin ... end;
  procedure Adapter.Correlate.yyy(...); begin ... end;
end.
```

Figure 6.12: PASCAL *skeleton an an adapter*

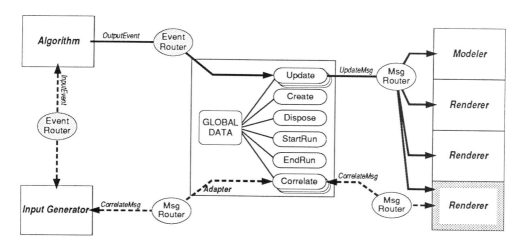

Figure 6.13: *Graphical representation of one type of adapter module*

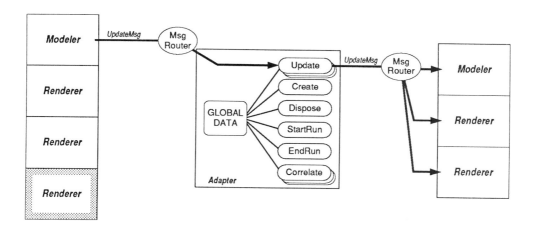

Figure 6.14: *Graphical representation of the other type of adapter module*

Modeler and Renderer Module

There is at most one modeler associated with each renderer, and in general, multiple renderers associated with each modeler. Modelers may be nested; nested modelers are called submodelers, and renderers may also be associated with them. The code skeleton and graphical representation show only a single renderer; neither shows any submodelers.

A modeler contains a collection of *Update* routines, and a renderer contains the same collection of *Update* routines and also a collection of *Correlate* routines. Each collection is represented by a single entry with a suffix *xxx* or *yyy* in the PASCAL code skeleton.

```
module Views;
  var ...;
  module Modeler;
    var ...;
    procedure Modeler.Create; begin ... end;
    procedure Modeler.Dispose; begin ... end;
    procedure Modeler.StartRun; begin ... end;
    procedure Modeler.EndRun; begin ... end;
    procedure Modeler.Update.xxx(...); begin ... end;
    end.
  module Renderer;
    var ...;
    procedure Renderer.Create; begin ... end;
    procedure Renderer.Dispose; begin ... end;
    procedure Renderer.StartRun; begin ... end;
    procedure Renderer.EndRun; begin ... end;
    procedure Renderer.Parms; begin ... end;
    procedure Renderer.Refresh; begin ... end;
    procedure Renderer.DID; begin ... end;
    procedure Renderer.Update.xxx(...); begin ... end;
    procedure Renderer.Correlate.yyy(...); begin ... end;
    end.
  end.
```

Figure 6.15: PASCAL *skeleton of a modeler with a single renderer.*

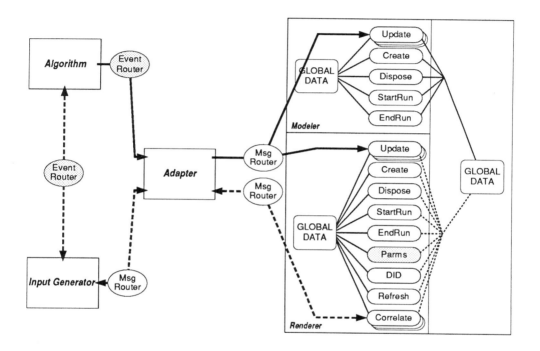

Figure 6.16: *Graphical representation of a modeler with a single renderer.*

6.4 Evaluation

Unfortunately, it is easy for a malicious client-programmer or script author to cause the BALSA–II system to behave strangely because control passes from the system to code implemented by client-programmers and script authors. The integrity of their code is beyond BALSA–II's control.

Non-malicious client-programmers can also cause problems, say, by using the wrong type of annotation or by annotating a subroutine that should not contain any annotations. BALSA–II does not currently check for such errors, although such problems can easily be caught at runtime. To do so, each glue routine would test that its caller, which it can inquire from the BALSA–II system, is of the correct type. Other errors are not so easy to catch. For example, novice client-programmers often erroneously use a renderer to update the modeler's data structures, a modeler to update a renderer's data structures, or chain onto a renderer rather than a modeler.

We have designed BALSA–II with considerable attention to portability. For instance, although BALSA–II is written using the Macintosh Toolkit, it uses only the common functions that are typically found in all workstation toolkits. Porting to another WSE would involve identifying the set of Macintosh Toolkit entries that BALSA–II uses and mapping those onto the similar entries in the target WSE. Perhaps the most serious problem is that displays in BALSA–II are written using QuickDraw. This further emphasizes the need to solidify the modeling package, since the modeling package isolates most of the view code from QuickDraw.

We have tried to limit non-graphical system dependencies as well. For instance, the only enhanced features of PASCAL that we utilize are separately compiled modules and coercing the datatype of pointers. Both of these features are found in virtually all PASCAL compilers. Coroutines, although they are typically not found in today's programming environments, are simple to implement. They are patterned after the UNIX *setjmp* and *longjmp* calls and require a half-dozen or so lines of assembly language code. Alternatively, since coroutines are used solely to simulate multiple processes, separate threads of control—if available—could be used. We will return to this idea in the next chapter. The one esoteric language feature that we do use are nested, reentrant modules. As we have shown, these effects can be simulated in a portable way by using a preprocessor and adhering to coding conventions.

Finally, we reemphasize that our design is conducive to implementing algorithms, input generators, and views in any of the object-oriented extensions to procedural languages. Doing so would require only minor and straightforward changes to the language-dependent parts of the preprocessor.

7

Conclusion

Algorithm animation crosses many disciplines, ranging from those highly technical to those purely aesthetic. Our research has concentrated on the technical aspects, of which there are many. Our model for constructing and interacting with animated algorithms and scripts has been realized in BALSA–I and BALSA–II. The model and prototype systems have proven to be well suited for animating scores of algorithms from many domains and has had demonstrated utility in a variety of interesting and important applications. Much more work remains to enable animated displays of programs and of other complex or abstract phenomena to become a mainstream component in computing environments. This chapter outlines areas for further research to help make this happen.

7.1 End-User Research Directions

"Real System" Integration

An algorithm animation environment, as we have described it, is not particularly well suited to tracing an algorithm line by line. The problem is that values of variables are not readily available, as they would be in an interpreter or debugger. Also, direct displays of the data structures are desirable when tracing algorithms. Such displays are tedious to construct in an algorithm animation system because annotations are required after virtually every statement. Moreover, as discussed in Chapter 1, direct displays of data structures can be, and hence, should be constructed automatically.

A naive solution is to run the algorithm animation environment under a traditional debugger. To an end-user (although the distinction between end-users and client-programmers becomes fuzzy at this point), the algorithm animation system would function as a compiled library; only client-programmer code would be available through the debugger. Such a solution, though functional, is not ideal. Minimally, the two ways to control execution, through the debugger or through the algorithm animation environment, will be confusing.

An integrated system is a goal worth striving for. Such a system would not only provide all of the program visualization displays described in Chapters 1 and 2 that can be created automatically, but would also have features found in modern programming environments for examining data and program states. Moreover, it could support the interpreter features of an algorithm animation environment for running programs together, and the window management features for controlling both the automatic views and the algorithm animation views in a consistent manner. The script facility described in Chapter 4 is easily extended to supporting typical interaction in a program development system. For instance, editing a program would be considered a structural property, and examining variables at run-time would be a presentation property. Changing a variable at run-time is analogous to responding to a runtime specific.

Attaching Views Interactively

In our prototype system, the set of potential views for an algorithm is fixed at run-time from information provided by the client-programmer. Consequently, the end-user cannot use any arbitrary view to see an algorithm, but is limited to a predefined collection. How could we allow end-users to use arbitrary views? One way is analogous to the way PROVIDE (see Chapter 2) allowed dynamic binding of program variables to display variables. In an algorithm animation system, the binding would be between program operations (i.e., algorithm events specified by the client-programmer) and the operations driving the display (i.e., update messages). In fact, such a strategy fits nicely into our current model in two ways. First, the mechanism for such a binding already exists in the form of an adapter. A "forms-oriented" interface to the adapter might be a reasonable way for end-users to specify the bindings. Second, once a binding is established, a wide collection of views (that is, those that are functionally similar and functionally equivalent, as defined in Chapter 5), becomes available because they will use the same binding.

Classifying Views

Already, a large number of different views have been developed and many
more are currently under development. With a large library of views come
both advantages and disadvantages. The advantage is that one can often use
an existing view instead of implementing one from scratch. The disadvantage is the difficulty of finding a view in the library based on its graphical
characteristics. Fortunately, graphical databases are an interesting research
topic independent of algorithm animation, although dynamic objects raise
additional issues that have not yet been addressed in the literature; progress
may well be made soon on this front as databases of dynamic objects become
commonplace.

Composing Views

A mundane but useful tool for end-users is one for building composite views.
In our model, each view window is independent of all other view windows.
In general, this design works out well. However, at times multiple views are
in fact related, and judicious placement of the windows can create a rich
composite picture. A simple tool would allow an end-user to specify "glue"
on the side or corner of a view window to attach two or more windows. A
similar effect could be achieved by dividing a window into internal panes.
The window dressing would control the contents of all of the attached view
windows. Another tool would allow multiple views to be drawn in the exact
same window. However, a problem intrinsic in this approach is that one
renderer might obscure parts of the image that another renderer is producing.

A special type of view composition, and one that is not difficult to implement, is to add a "transcript" pad to the window. Such a feature is
analogous to the scrollable transcript of an end-user's session contained by
most workstations. In our application, an end-user would specify which algorithm event would cause a copy of the view to be saved in the transcript
pad. Simple extensions, such as allowing the end-user to specify how the
composition should be arranged (e.g., horizontally, vertically, checkerboard)
could produce a very effective story of how an algorithm progressed.

A much more difficult issue (one for which a solution may well not even
exist) involves coordinating the graphical cues in various windows. Thus,
if one view used a particular highlighting technique to represent something,
then other views should use the same highlighting technique to mean the
same thing. Achieving this goal is easy for renderers based on the same

modeler. However, tools are needed so that diverse views, written by different people at different times and with different purposes, can be used together harmoniously. Part of the solution involves creating a semiology of animated program displays.

7.2 Animator Research Directions

Interleaving Smooth Animations

In our model, views are updated sequentially at each algorithm event. More specifically, first the adapters are called, then the modelers (this might involve calling other adapters because of chained modelers), and finally the renderers are called to update the image in each view window. When each view is updated discretely and the update happens quickly, this strategy is successful. However, when a view is updated incrementally, the sequential nature of the updates becomes noticeable and problematic: while smooth animation is taking place, all other views on the screen are noticeably idle. This problem is acute when multiple algorithms each have multiple incremental views.

A standard solution is to provide an animation package. Each renderer, rather than making graphics calls directly, would register the requests with the animation package. After all renderers have registered their requests, the algorithm animation system would notify the animation packages to perform the incremental updates. A somewhat subtle advantage to this approach is that the end-user's notion of the cost associated with each event could be better displayed: the algorithm animation system would specify to the animation package how much time each update should consume.

Unfortunately, although animation packages have received considerable attention in the computer graphics literature for well over two decades, real-time performance on "modest" hardware is another issue. Ideally, a rich graphics package such as POSTSCRIPT could be implemented to yield real-time performance, and could then be extended for animation and for color.

WYSIWYG Animations

An interesting research problem is to see how close one could come to eliminating the animator. Paint systems and structured drawing systems provide, in some sense, graphical direct-manipulation WYSIWYG interfaces to program-callable graphics packages; to what extent and with what level of sophistication can animations be constructed in an analogous WYSIWYG fashion? Because algorithm displays are, in general, quite detailed, one would probably want to have available both a programming language description and a visual description of the animation. Moreover, one would like to use either description for editing, and changes made in one should be immediately displayed in the other. Research is underway to investigate such a "double viewing" paradigm, but only for static images [3].

Advanced Hardware

More advanced hardware will certainly affect an animator's job, and with it will come new challenges. For example, color allows more information to be presented, though indiscriminate use of it often hinders, not helps, the viewer. Hardware now routinely includes sophisticated sound capabilities. Like color, sound has the potential to show intricate patterns and relationships among many variables. It is, perhaps, even more difficult than color to use effectively, however, especially since many "viewers" are tone-deaf. Preliminary experiments indicate that multiple views each with sound quickly remind viewers of Manhattan at rush hour. Some interesting uses of sound for analyzing data, among other applications, can be found elsewhere [19].

More sophisticated hardware will also make possible real-time animation of three-dimensional (or more) color representations of algorithms. Of course, this will involve building a sophisticated modeling package to handle such objects. The software to implement a modeling package will be easy (and packages are available in numerous research laboratories) when compared to the task of using it in a meaningful way.

Leading figures in the visual displays of information, such as Tufte [67] and Bertin [12, 13], have not addressed the issues that advanced hardware seem destined to raise. To what extent do their principals scale? Computer scientists will surely need to team with graphic designers to exploit the advanced hardware.

Scripts

Hardware improvements also create many new possibilities for using scripts, some of which we mentioned in Chapter 4. For example, very high-resolution monitors (300 dots per inch) are now available whose resolution rival that of the printed page. Research in electronic documents until now has, undoubtedly been influenced by the relatively low-resolution monitors available. How practical is an "electronic document" now, and how do text and dynamic diagrams coexist? CD-ROMS will also affect scripts and other forms of electronic documents.

Generalizing scripts beyond algorithm animation is a challenging problem. What types of applications are characterized by structural, temporal, and presentation properties? What type are not, and why not? What types of properties characterize other systems? How do these integrate into our notion of customizable videotapes?

7.3 Systems Research Directions

Virtually all of the issues mentioned thus far have strong implications for systems research. Multiple processes, discussed in this section, seems directed solely to the "systems guru" building an algorithm animation system.

Multiple Processes

There are a number of ways that we could use multiple processes rather than a single thread of execution, either on one machine or on multiple processors. The most obvious way is to assign each "module" (e.g., an algorithm, input generator, adapter, modeler and renderer) as its own process. This would have the advantage of greatly simplifying parts of the preprocessing phase, since each module would be in its own address space. Preliminary experiments reveal two problems. First, the granularity of the operating system's scheduler is sufficiently large that the updates of the views appear to be sequential. Second, because modelers and renderers (as well as submodelers) share data, in addition to their own data, some additional low-level system-specific coding is needed to share and synchronize data for applications operating in parallel.

Regardless of these problems, our design is easily adaptable to different configurations of processes. If many processes are available, we assign each module to its own process, as mentioned above. Using animation package for interleaving the graphic calls for various views, as described earlier in this chapter, the problems concerning the granularity of the operating system's scheduler are solved. If fewer processes are available, the approach is modified as follows: (1) Let all algorithms advance in parallel until their next event. (2) Let all modelers operate in parallel. Actually, submodelers must wait until their parent modelers have finished. (3) Let all renderers update together in parallel, assuming that multiple processes can access the screen simultaneously.

7.4 Final Thoughts

Every reader will remember something different about this thesis. Some might remember a handful of the screen images portraying the workings of familiar algorithms (ones that they had perhaps not fully understood before); others might remember our two-page, language-independent "interpreter" that executes compiled code; still others might only remember our models of object-oriented pipes or of scripts. While these pictures, hacks, and conceptual ideas are, perhaps, interesting and innovative, they are not the essence of this dissertation.

This dissertation is about what graphics-based workstations can be, and indeed should be. They are more than merely a collection of terminals. A picture is worth a thousand words, a movie even more. But interactive movies, available on workstations to virtually everybody, are even more valuable. The difficulty in future years will not be a lack of hardware; it will be lack of software, and the lack of creative visual thinking to drive new software. If this thesis is successful, then it will contribute to its being looked upon in years to come as but a primitive attempt to harness computer hardware as an aid for understanding and thinking about complex phenomena.

Appendix A

An Electronic Classroom

The Foxboro Auditorium lecture hall at Brown University, designed in 1982, houses a network of high-performance workstations. Since September, 1983, the lab has been equipped with 55 Apollo DN300 workstations featuring a Motorola 68010 processor with 1.5MB of main memory. There is an additional 128KB of memory dedicated to the $1024 \times 800 \times 1$ resolution bit-mapped display, and a hardware "Bit-Blt" capable of moving rectangular regions of memory at the rate of 32 Mbits per second. Each machine has a 3-button mouse for graphical input, and groups of four machines share a 158MB Winchester disk attached to a DN400 server. All nodes are connected by the Apollo DOMAIN, a high-bandwidth local-area network.

The primary goal of Brown's "Electronic Classroom" project, started in June, 1980, was to explore how the computer could be used to complement the instructor by providing a unique (at that time) and innovative medium of communication. Rather than using chalkboards or viewgraphs to show static diagrams—often incorrectly drawn and messy at best—or asking teaching assistants to become Thespians in order to "enact" procedure calls, searching and sorting algorithms, traveling salesmen, and so forth, dynamic simulations of the algorithms and programming concepts are presented via the workstations. Moreover, instructors and students can interact with these "movies" to gain an even better insight into the intricacies of the new concepts.

The introductory programming course for computer science majors and the third-semester algorithms course have been using the facility since the fall of 1983. Both courses have now been taught four times (with refinements of the animations and to the BALSA–I environment each year), and have developed very different styles of operation. In addition, computer science courses in graphics and assembly language programming, and mathematics courses in differential equations and differential geometry use the Electronic Classroom on a regular basis.

The Introductory Programming Course

In the introductory programming course, the instructor usually spends the first half of class in "broadcast" mode: everything displayed on his screen appears simultaneously on each student's. The instructor can use a large software cursor on his screen (which also is seen on each student's screen) to focus attention on a particular part of the screen. Algorithms and graphical views must be prepared in advance and cannot be changed during class. However, the instructor has the flexibility to run and rerun the program with arbitrary data interactively, and change the size, location, and contents of any of the view windows, and can gear the pace to the progress of the class. Most importantly, arbitrary "what-if" questions from students can be answered on the spot, graphically and thus convincingly, without the inevitable messy-blackboard syndrome.

In the second half of class, students usually try out programs at their own pace and with their own data. Undergraduate teaching assistants are available during this portion of class to assist with technical and conceptual problems. It is worth mentioning that while the initial plans called for one machine per student, because of monetary considerations and the physical size of the machines, each machine has ended up being shared by two students during class. This turned out to be an asset: "we found that students enjoyed working together and helped each other understand what was going on. Often there is a background murmur during the laboratory/lecture; this takes a bit of getting used to, but is apparently educationally effective" [69].

Another aspect of the initial plans was that students would during class modify the programs that had been presented by the instructor. For example, if the instructor was teaching linked lists and showing an algorithm to add an element to the end of the list, he might then ask students to modify the code so that the algorithm deleted the last element of the list. These plans never materialized, for two reasons. First, there just is not enough class time. It would require at least 20 to 30 minutes for the students to complete or modify the instructor's code; class time is already too short for just lectures and demos (both instructor-led and self-paced). Second, the BALSA–I software environment cannot take an arbitrary program and animate it automatically; rather, the algorithm must be augmented with annotations. It is certainly not reasonable to ask introductory students to deal with this complication; typically, they are having enough difficulties understanding the very basics of programming. Indeed, a major focus of this thesis has been to study this "magic," to understand it better, and to simplify it.

The Algorithms and Data Structures Course

In the algorithms course, each student's workstation replayed a "script" of the material that was previously created and saved. At key points, the script would cause the system to pause and wait for the student to continue when signaled by the instructor. The instructor would typically design his lecture as a play-by-play commentary on the simulations. There is rarely enough class time to let students run programs on their own or with their own data; however, the machines with scripts are available during non-class hours for students to do their programming assignments and investigate the simulations presented during class. Because each lecture corresponded directly to a chapter from the textbook [60], the scripts formed a very effective "dynamic book" accompaniment.

The student assignments were also integrated with the animated algorithms. For a variety of reasons, some technical and some not, student assignments were programmed using the native Apollo environment rather than the BALSA–I system. Provided with each programming assignment was a list of subroutines that students could insert into their code in order to display a graphical animation of their program. For example, an assignment on the Josephus problem ("N people sitting in a circle of whom every Mth is executed") might have an entry

   JosephusInit(N: Integer)

to draw a picture of N hollow "dots" arranged in a circle, and an entry

   JosephusDeath(k: Integer)

to fill and cross out the kth dot. Not too surprisingly, the graphics subroutines for an assignment matched the algorithm output events in the BALSA–I animations that were used in lectures for the corresponding material.

The flavor of the animations in the algorithms course was significantly different from those in the introductory programming course. The displays tended to have many views, and each view tended to be much more intricate. Emphasis was placed on running algorithms on large data sets to help students to form an intuition for what the algorithm does, and also on racing variants of an algorithm and different algorithms that do the same thing. In fact, examinations in the course included some "name-that-algorithm" pictures. Students who attended class found those problems very easy; they tended to remember and understand how the algorithm worked by the images of the dynamics of one (or more) of the views.

Other Courses

A number of other courses also use Foxboro Auditorium, though to a lesser extent. The graduate-level graphics course uses the BALSA–I system to demonstrate a number of the more difficult algorithms, such as polygon scan conversion, polygon clipping, and hidden surface removal, that are covered in the textbook [28]. Because of the sophistication of the students, the style of operation in this course is to let the students loose with the system to experiment with the algorithms at their own pace. At the other end of the curriculum, the second-semester programming course covering Motorola 68000 assembly language uses demonstrations in BALSA–I to illustrate the workings of the 68000 microprocessor. The animations typically show views of the data, address, and status registers, the accumulator, the memory (code and data), and the addressing modes. Because of the nature of the material, the displays tend to be textual and straightforward; nevertheless, student questionnaires almost uniformly indicate that they learn better in the "computer-assisted hand-simulation" classes and enjoy them more.

The Electronic Classroom is also in use by courses outside of computer science. An introductory neural science course developed a system that displays a model of the brain that can be rotated and zoomed in three dimensions. Mathematics courses on differential geometry and complex analysis use a system to display curves and surfaces, allowing students to set viewing specifications and parameters of the equations defining the objects. And finally, a differential equations course in the applied mathematics department used BALSA–I to build the PHASER system for displaying views of the graphs of difference and differential equations.

BALSA–I has also been used as a general-purpose simulation language for experiments by the Institute for Research in Information and Scholarship (IRIS) at Brown in a number of disciplines. These include physics experiments in gravity and springs, and a dynamic questionnaire concerning nuclear war. Programmers at IRIS also built some general-purpose CAI-like facilities on top of BALSA–I and used them for lessons in geography and linguistics. While these unanticipated uses of BALSA–I indicate that its basic framework and implementation are solid, the experiments indicated that some additional system support is needed for CAI-oriented lessons. Thus, we merely mention them in passing; Appendix B cites relevant literature documenting these applications.

Some Observations

Most courses supplement the dynamic presentations with a traditional view-graph and blackboard. This also provides an additional focus for the class as a whole. No formal studies have been made to compare the many ways that instructors used the dynamic media, nor can we do so here. It is interesting to note that the two courses completely organized around the animated algorithms, the Introductory Programming developed by van Dam, and Algorithms and Data Structures developed by Sedgewick, have settled on two very different styles. Comparing and contrasting these two styles is akin to evaluating a blackboard and a viewgraph: can we say that one is pedagogically "better" than the other?

The broadcast method used in the Introductory Programming course has the advantage of modifying the course of instruction to the pace of the class, but has the disadvantage of "pulling the rug out from under the students" when the instructor goes on to a new part of the animation. It also has the drawback that the instructor must be very familiar with the system and must interact with it extensively "under pressure." This method also had a higher incidence of technical problems, since it relies very heavily on the network,† while also exercising it extensively.

---

† It is not possible to connect the video input of one workstations to the video output of another workstation's.

The scripting method used in the Algorithms and Data Structures course has the advantage of allowing each pair of students some flexibility over the pace of the lecture. If a particular part of the animation is clear, they can advance a bit beyond the class, and they are also able to linger a bit on difficult sections. Scripting has the disadvantage that it is more difficult to prepare: an instructor must plan out his lecture carefully (and stick to the plan!). In practice, this often has the side-effect of producing more coherent and effective lectures. The pauses in the script have the side-effect of keeping the students involved by forcing them to advance the machine from one scene to the next. Scripts also provide a convenient starting point for self-study, because the sets of windows and data that were used in class are available and can be modified easily.

One might wonder whether scripts in the classroom are superior or even inferior to, say, a videotape or a videodisk, assuming that all students had their own monitors. Because scripts in BALSA–I are completely passive, there is little difference in the classroom. The advantage comes when one considers how easy it is to create and edit—even in BALSA–I—a script, and that students can use them later as a self-study guide. The scripts in BALSA–II are significantly different from and far superior to a videotape or videodisk because they can be interactively customized by the viewer. As new hardware becomes available (e.g., CD–ROMs and LaserWriter-quality screens), new and exciting avenues will be open for educators to explore.

Even though Foxboro Auditorium contains large-screen projection equipment, instructors uniformly refused to use it for lectures. In the introductory programming course, the instructor used a large software cursor to focus the class's attention on a particular part of the screen; in the algorithms course, the instructor pointed on his screen, which was turned to face the students. Instructors contended that darkening the room made for very cold and formal classes, in addition to the fact that it is very difficult for students to see details on projected screen images. In particular, instructors in the introductory class felt that the class was made "more immediate and intimate" by not using a single projected workstation; in addition, it made the transition to "run it yourself" (the second half of class) much easier.

The bottom-line question the Electronic Classroom raises is "Do the simulations help?" Unfortunately, no controlled experiments could be done to answer this credibly. Instructors in the courses were able to cover material at a much accelerated rate (estimated at 30% faster); however, the introduction of the lab coincided with the introduction of formal textbooks for both courses. As many universities are building electronic classrooms of their own and equipping them with workstations as powerful as those in Foxboro Auditorium—but at a fraction of the cost—experiments are sure to be done to answer this and other interesting pedagogical questions that arise from the new technology.

Appendix B

BALSA-Related Publications

Videotapes

- *Algorithm Animation Sampler*, 10-minute black-and-white silent video-tape, Dept. of Computer Science, Brown University, Providence, RI, July 1984. Shown at *SIGGRAPH '84* in conjunction with [17].

- *Animated Graphics Algorithms*, 10-minute black-and-white sound video-tape, Dept. of Computer Science, Brown University, Providence, RI, May 1986. Corresponds to various parts of [28].

- *Progress Report: Brown University Instructional Computing Laboratory*, 23-minute color sound videotape, Dept. of Computer Science, Brown University, Providence, RI, December 1983. Shown at *SIGCSE '84* in conjunction with [16].

Technical Reports

- L. NANCY GARRETT, JANINE A. ROETH, KAREN E. SMITH, AND ELISABETH A. WAYMIRE. "The Sampler Program Descriptions," *IRIS Technical Report*, Brown University, Providence, RI, April 1985.

- L. NANCY GARRETT AND MATT P. EVETT. "Notes on Writing Educational Software in the BALSA Environment," *Technical Report IRIS–85–2*, Brown University, Providence, RI, May 1985.

- HÜSEYIN KOÇAK, MATTHEW A. MERZBACHER, AND MICHAEL D. STRICKMAN. "Dynamical Systems with Computer Experiments at the Brown University Instructional Computing Laboratory," *Technical Report CS–84–14*, Brown University, Providence, RI, June 1984. See also: HÜSEYIN KOÇAK. *Differential and Difference Equations Through Computer Experiments,* Springer-Verlag, New York, 1986.

- KAREN E. SMITH. "Developing and Evaluating A Computer-Assisted Instruction Dialogue on Parameters," *Technical Report CS–85–4* Brown University, Providence, RI, February 1985.

- KAREN E. SMITH AND ELISABETH A. WAYMIRE. "Brown University's Computerized Classroom: An Experiment in the Principles of Courseware Design," *Technical Report CS–84–18*, Brown University, Providence, RI, October 1984.

- NICOLE YANKELOVICH, L. NANCY GARRETT, JANINE A. ROETH, KAREN E. SMITH, AND ELISABETH A. WAYMIRE. "The Sampler Companion," *Technical Report IRIS–85–1*, Brown University, Providence, RI, January 1985.

Journals and Conference Proceedings

The [number] indicates a citation in the References.

- MARC H. BROWN, NORMAN K. MEYROWITZ, AND ANDRIES VAN DAM. "Personal Computer Networks and Graphical Animation: Rationale and Practice for Education," *ACM SIGCSE Bulletin*, **15**, 1 (February 1983), 296–307.

[16] MARC H. BROWN AND ROBERT SEDGEWICK. "Progress Report: Brown University Instructional Computing Laboratory," *ACM SIGCSE Bulletin*, **16**, 1 (February 1984), 91–101.

[17] MARC H. BROWN AND ROBERT SEDGEWICK. "A System for Algorithm Animation," *Computer Graphics*, **18**, 3 (July 1984), 177–186.

[18] MARC H. BROWN AND ROBERT SEDGEWICK. "Techniques for Algorithm Animation," *IEEE Software*, **2**, 1 (January 1985), 28–39.

- WILLIAM S. SHIPP, NORMAN K. MEYROWITZ, AND ANDRIES VAN DAM. "Networks of Scholar's Workstations in a University Community," *IEEE COMPCON Fall '83*, 108–122.

[69] ANDRIES VAN DAM. "The Electronic Classroom: Workstations for Teaching," *International Journal of Man-Machine Studies*, **21**, 4 (October 1984), 353–363.

[73] NICOLE YANKELOVICH, NORMAN K. MEYROWITZ, AND ANDRIES VAN DAM. "Reading and Writing the Electronic Book," *IEEE Computer*, **18**, 10 (October 1985), 15–30.

References

[1] JIM ANDERSON, GEORGE BOSWORTH, ALBERTO A. DELLA RIPA, BARBARA NOPARSTAK, AND MICHAEL TENG. *Method's Owners Manual*, Digitalk Inc., Los Angeles, CA, 1985.

[2] APPLE COMPUTER, INC. *Inside Macintosh*, Addison-Wesley, Reading, MA, 1985.

[3] PAUL ASENTE. "Editing Procedural Description of Graphical Objects," *Abstracts and Viewgraphs from the 19th Annual Meeting of the Stanford Computer Forum*, February 1987, 229–234. An abstract of the author's Ph.D. dissertation in progress. Working title of thesis is: *Editing Graphical Objects using Procedural Representations*.

[4] ANIL BAJAJ, KELLY HICKMAN, THOMAS A. STANDISH. *Guide to the MiniAda and SmallGol Visible Compilers*, Andromeda, 3018 Mountain View Dr., Laguna Beach, CA, 1986.

[5] ROBERT M. BALZER. "EXDAMS—EXtendable Debugging and Monitoring System," *Proc. AFIPS Spring Joint Computer Conf.*, 1969, 567–580.

[6] RONALD M. BAECKER. "Towards Animating Computer Programs: A First Progress Report," *Proc. 3rd Canadian National Research Council's Man-Computer Communications Seminar*, May 1973, 4.1–4.10.

[7] RONALD M. BAECKER. "Two System Which Produce Animated Representations of the Execution of Computer Programs," *ACM SIGCSE Bulletin*, **7**, 1 (February 1975), 158–167.

[8] RONALD M. BAECKER. "An Application Overview of Program Visualization," *Computer Graphics*, **20**, 4 (July 1986), 325.

[9] RONALD M. BAECKER AND DAVID SHERMAN. *Sorting Out Sorting*, 16mm color sound film, 30 minutes, 1981. (Shown at *ACM SIGGRAPH '81* in Dallas, TX and excerpted in *ACM SIGGRAPH Video Review* #7, 1983.)

[10] DAVID B. BASKERVILLE. "Graphic Presentation of Data Structures in the DBX Debugger," *Report No. UCB/CSD 86/260*, University of California at Berkeley, Berkeley, CA, October 1985.

[11] JON L. BENTLEY AND BRIAN W. KERNIGHAN. "A System for Algorithm Animation: Tutorial and User Manual," *Computer Science Technical Report No. 132*, AT&T Bell Laboratories, Murray Hill, NJ, January 1987.

[12] JACQUES BERTIN. *Graphics and Graphic Information Processing*, de Gruyter, Berlin, 1981. Translated from *La Graphique et le Traitement Graphique de l'Information* (1977) by William J. Berg and Paul Scott.

[13] JACQUES BERTIN. *Semiology of Graphics*, University of Wisconsin Press, Madison, WI, 1983. Translated from *Sémilogie Graphique* (1973 edition) by William J. Berg.

[14] KELLOG S. BOOTH. *PQ Trees*, 16mm color silent film, 12 minutes, 1975.

[15] GRETCHEN P. BROWN, RICHARD T. CARLING, CHRISTOPHER F. HEROT, DAVID A. KRAMLICH, AND PAUL SOUZA. "Program Visualization: Graphical Support for Software Development," *IEEE Computer*, **18**, 8 (August 1985), 27–35.

[16] MARC H. BROWN AND ROBERT SEDGEWICK. "Progress Report: Brown University Instructional Computing Laboratory," *ACM SIGCSE Bulletin*, **16**, 1 (February 1984), 91–101.

[17] MARC H. BROWN AND ROBERT SEDGEWICK. "A System for Algorithm Animation," *Computer Graphics*, **18**, 3 (July 1984), 177–186.

[18] MARC H. BROWN AND ROBERT SEDGEWICK. "Techniques for Algorithm Animation," *IEEE Software*, **2**, 1 (January 1985), 28–39.

[19] WILLIAM BUXTON. "Communicating with Sound," *Proc. ACM SIGCHI '85 Conf. on Human Factors in Computing Systems*, April 1985, 115–119. Members of this panel session were S. Bly, S. P. Frysinger, D. Lunney, D. L. Mansur, J. J. Mezrich, and R. C. Morrison

[20] SHI-KUO CHANG. "Visual Languages: A Tutorial and Survey," *IEEE Software*, **4**, 1 (January 1987), 29–39.

[21] SHI-KUO CHANG, TADAO ICHIKAWA, AND PANOS A. LIGOMENIDES, Editors. *Visual Languages*, Plenum Press, New York, 1986.

[22] JAMES M. DE BOER. *A System for the Animation of Micro-PL/I Programs*, M.Sc.Thesis, Dept. of Computer Science, University of Toronto, Toronto, ON, 1974.

[23] ROBERT A. DUISBERG. *Constraint-Based Animation: Temporal Constraints in the Animus System*, Ph.D.Thesis, Computer Science Department, University of Washington, Seattle, WA, 1986. Also available as Technical Report 86-09-01.

[24] ROBERT A. DUISBERG. "Animated Graphical Interfaces Using Temporal Constraints," *Proc. ACM SIGCHI '86 Conf. on Human Factors in Computing Systems*, April 1986, 131–136.

[25] STEVEN K. FEINER. "APEX: An Experiment in the Automated Creation of Pictorial Explanations," *IEEE Computer Graphics and Applications*, **5**, 11 (November 1985), 29–37.

[26] STEVEN K. FEINER, SANDOR NAGY, AND ANDRIES VAN DAM. "An Experimental System for Creating and Presenting Interactive Graphical Documents," *ACM Trans. on Graphics*, **1**, 1 (January 1982), 59–77.

[27] JAMES D. FOLEY AND CHARLES F. MCMATH. "Dynamic Process Visualization," *IEEE Computer Graphics and Applications*, **6**, 3 (March 1986), 16–25.

[28] JAMES D. FOLEY AND ANDRIES VAN DAM. *Fundamentals of Interactive Computer Graphics*, Addison-Wesley, Reading, MA, 1982.

[29] MICHAEL L. FREDMAN, ROBERT SEDGEWICK, DANIEL D. SLEATOR, AND ROBERT E. TARJAN. "The Pairing Heap: A New Form of Self-Adjusting Heap," *Algorithmica*, **1**, 1 (1986), 111–129.

[30] ADELE GOLDBERG. "Why Smalltalk is not for children: issues of handling complexity in the software system," *Transcript of a talk presented at ECOO '82*, 1982, 13–16.

[31] ADELE GOLDBERG AND DAVID ROBSON. *Smalltalk-80: The Language and its Implementation*, Addison-Wesley, Reading, MA, 1983.

[32] ROBERT B. GRAFTON AND TADAO ICHIKAWA. "Visual Programming: Guest Editors' Introduction," *IEEE Computer*, **18**, 8 (August 1985), 6–9.

[33] DANIEL C. HALBERT. "Programming by Example," *OSD–T8402*, Xerox OSD, Palo Alto, CA, 1984.

[34] CHRISTOPHER F. HEROT. "Spatial Management of Data," *ACM Trans. on Database Systems*, **5**, 4 (December 1980), 493–514.

[35] CHRISTOPHER F. HEROT, GRETCHEN P. BROWN, RICHARD T. CARLING, MARK FRIEDEL, DAVID KRAMLICH, AND RONALD M. BAECKER. "An Integrated Environment for Program Visualization," in H. J. Schneider and A. I. Wasserman, Eds., *Automated Tools for Information Systems Design*, North Holland Publishing Co., 1982, 237–259.

[36] ZHU HONG AND ROBERT SEDGEWICK. "Notes on Merging Networks," *Proc. of the 14th Annual ACM Symp. on Theory of Computing*, May, 1982, 296–302.

[37] F. ROBERT A. HOPGOOD. "Computer Animation Used as a Tool in Teaching Computer Science," *Proc. 1974 IFIP Congress*, 1974, 889–892.

[38] WILLIAM H. HUGGINS. "Iconic Communications," *IEEE Trans. on Education*, **E–14**, 4 (November 1971), 158–163.

[39] WILLIAM H. HUGGINS AND DORIS R. ENTWISLE. "Computer Animation for the Academic Community," *Proc. 1969 Spring Joint Computer Conf.*, 1969, 623–627.

[40] "Hypermedia Bibliography," *Institute for Research in Information and Scholarship (IRIS)*, Brown University, Providence, RI, March 1987.

[41] JANET M. INCERPI. *A Study of the Worst-Case Behavior of Shellsort*, Ph.D. Thesis, Computer Science Department, Brown University, Providence, RI, 1986.

[42] KENNETH C. KNOWLTON. *L6: Bell Telephone Laboratories Low-Level Linked List Language*, two 16mm black and white sound films, 1966.

[43] DONALD E. KNUTH. "Dynamic Huffman Coding," *Journal of Algorithms*, **6**, 2 (June 1985), 163–180.

[44] DAVID A. KRAMLICH, GRETCHEN P. BROWN, RICHARD T. CARLING, AND CHRISTOPHER F. HEROT. "Program Visualization: Graphics Support for Software Development," *Proc. ACM/IEEE 20th Design Automation Conf.*, 1983, 143–149.

[45] STEVE LAMBERT AND SUZANNE ROPIEQUET, Editors. *CD/ROM: The New Papyrus*, Microsoft Press, Redmond, WA, 1986.

[46] RICHARD J. LIPTON, STEVEN C. NORTH, AND J. S. SANDBERG. "How to Draw a Graph," *Proc. of the Symp. on Computational Geometry*, June 1985, 153–160.

[47] RALPH L. LONDON AND ROBERT A. DUISBERG. "Animating Programs Using Smalltalk," *IEEE Computer*, **18**, 8 (August 1985), 61–71.

[48] JOCK MACKINLAY. "Automated Creation of Illustrations for Technical Publications," *ACM Siggraph '86 Tutorial Course Notes*, Dallas, TX, August, 1986.

[49] MITCHELL L. MODEL. "Monitoring System Behavior In a Complex Computational Environment," *CSL–79–1*, Xerox PARC, Palo Alto, CA, 1979.

[50] THOMAS G. MOHER. "PROVIDE: a Process Visualization and Debugging Environment," *Technical Report*, University of Illinois at Chicago, Chicago, IL, July 1985.

[51] BRAD A. MYERS. "Displaying Data Structures for Interactive Debugging," *CSL–80–7*, Xerox PARC, Palo Alto, CA, 1980.

[52] BRAD A. MYERS. "Incense: A System for Displaying Data Structures," *Computer Graphics*, **17**, 3 (July 1983), 115–125.

[53] BRAD A. MYERS. "Visual Programming, Programming by Example, and Program Visualization: A Taxonomy," *Proc. ACM SIGCHI '86 Conf. on Human Factors in Computing Systems*, April 1986, 59–66.

[54] BERNHARD PLATTNER AND JURG NIEVERGELT. "Monitoring Program Execution: A Survey," *Computer*, **14**, 11 (November 1981), 76–93.

[55] GEORG RAEDER. "A Survey of Current Graphical Programming Techniques," *IEEE Computer*, **18**, 8 (August 1985), 11–25.

[56] EDWARD M. REINGOLD AND JOHN S. TILFORD. "Tidier Drawings of Trees," *IEEE Trans. on Software Engineering*, **SE–7**, 2 (March 1981), 223–228.

[57] STEVEN P. REISS. "A Framework for Graphical Programming (Summary Paper)," *Technical Report*, Brown University, Providence, RI, August 1985.

[58] STEVEN P. REISS. "GARDEN: An Environment for Graphical Programming," *Technical Report*, Brown University, Providence, RI, October 1985.

[59] STEVEN P. REISS. "Displaying Program and Data Structures," *Technical Report CS–86–19*, Brown University, Providence, RI, April 1986.

[60] ROBERT SEDGEWICK. *Algorithms*, Addison-Wesley, Reading, MA, 1983.

[61] ROBERT SEDGEWICK AND JEFFREY S. VITTER. "Shortest Paths in Euclidean Graphs," *Proc. 25th Annual Symp. on the Foundations of Computer Science*, October 1984, 417–424.

[62] MARK J. STEFIK, DANIEL G. BOBROW, AND KENNETH M. KAHN. "Integrating Access-Oriented Programming into a Multiparadigm Environment," *IEEE Software*, **3**, 1 (January 1986), 10–18.

[63] WILLIAM STRUNK JR. AND E. B. WHITE. *The Elements of Style,* 3rd Ed., Macmillan Publishing Co., Inc., New York, NY, 1979.

[64] WARREN TEITELMAN. "A Display Oriented Programmer's Assistant," *CSL–77–3*, Xerox PARC, Palo Alto, CA, March 1977.

[65] WARREN TEITELMAN. "A Tour Through Cedar," *IEEE Software*, **1**, 2 (April 1984), 44–73.

[66] LARRY TESLER. "The Smalltalk Environment," *BYTE*, **6**, 8 (August 1981), 90–147. This entire issue of *BYTE* is devoted to the Smalltalk language, environment, and experience.

[67] EDWARD R. TUFTE. *The Visual Display of Quantitative Information*, Graphics Press, Cheshire, CT, 1983.

[68] UNIPRESS SOFTWARE, INC. *UniPress EMACS Screen Editor: User's Guide and Unix Reference Manual*, Edison, NJ, 1986.

[69] ANDRIES VAN DAM. "The Electronic Classroom: Workstations for Teaching," *International Journal of Man-Machine Studies*, **21**, 4 (October 1984), 353–363.

[70] JEFFREY S. VITTER. "Design and Analysis of Dynamic Huffman Coding," *Proc. 26th Annual Symp. on the Foundations of Computer Science*, October 1985, 293–302.

[71] CHARLES WETHERELL AND ALFRED SHANNON. "Tidy Drawings of Trees," *IEEE Trans. on Software Engineering*, **SE–5**, 5 (Sept. 1979), 514–520.

[72] STEPHEN A. WEYER AND ALAN H. BORNING. "A Prototype Electronic Encyclopedia," *ACM Trans. on Office Information Systems*, **3**, 1 (January 1985), 63–88.

[73] NICOLE YANKELOVICH, NORMAN K. MEYROWITZ, AND ANDRIES VAN DAM. "Reading and Writing the Electronic Book," *IEEE Computer*, **18**, 10 (October 1985), 15–30.

[74] EDWARD YARWOOD. *Toward Program Illustration*, M.Sc.Thesis, Dept. of Computer Science, University of Toronto, Toronto, ON, 1974.

Index

The [*number*] indicates a citation in the References.

The MIT Press, with Peter Denning, general consulting editor, and Brian Randell, European consulting editor, publishes computer science books in the following series:

ACM Doctoral Dissertation Award and Distinguished Dissertation Series

Artificial Intelligence, Patrick Winston and Michael Brady, editors

Charles Babbage Institute Reprint Series for the History of Computing, Martin Campbell-Kelly, editor

Computer Systems, Herb Schwetman, editor

Exploring with Logo, E. Paul Goldenberg, editor

Foundations of Computing, Michael Garey and Albert Meyer, editors

History of Computing, I. Bernard Cohen and William Aspray, editors

Information Systems, Michael Lesk, editor

Logic Programming, Ehud Shapiro, editor; Fernando Pereira, Koichi Furukawa, and D. H. D. Warren, associate editors

The MIT Electrical Engineering and Computer Science Series

Scientific Computation, Dennis Gannon, editor